BEYOND THE BOULEVARDS

A SHORT BIOGRAPHY OF

PONDICHERRY

÷

ADITI SRIRAM

ALEPH

ALEPH

ALEPH BOOK COMPANY
An independent publishing firm
promoted by *Rupa Publications India*

First published in India in 2019
by Aleph Book Company
7/16 Ansari Road, Daryaganj
New Delhi 110 002

ISBN: 978-93-88292-46-7

1 3 5 7 9 10 8 6 4 2

Printed and bound in India by Replika Press Pvt. Ltd.

To my grandparents,
and the houses they built

Contents

Prologue: A Game of Pétanque

As 6 p.m. nears, a group of men has assembled in their corner of Joan of Arc Park, divided into teams, looking serious. One of them rolls a small wooden ball onto the pitch. The two teams then take turns throwing their boules, which are heavier, metallic balls, as close to the wooden one as they can. Men in dark red-and-blue tracksuits stand, crouch, bend, test the ground in the park's northeast corner where the grass has been worn thin by the daily roll of these weighty balls. Their uniforms announce polysyllabic South Indian names dressed up in European vowels and accents. Péroumal. Soubaraw. Aroumougam. Mouttoucomarassamy.

Pétanque is a measured game, a few-hundred-year-old French sport that mixes the daintiness of croquet with the precision of carom and the heft of bowling. Children crane their necks over the park wall to watch. They follow the arc of the player's arm as he simultaneously stretches and twists it before releasing the ball. Against the backdrop of waves, conversation, and calls to prayer, the game asserts itself with a tok-tok as one team's boule strikes another's away from the wooden ball. The struck wordlessly studies the striker's throw. His teammate squats and squints, examining what to do next. He aims and throws, but in vain; the boules do not make contact. The others titter, take a few paces; the gathered pedestrians shift about and turn to the setting sun to check the time. They resume their evening walk a few minutes later while the players, unaffected by their loss of audience, reorganize themselves. Theirs is a slow choreography which will only be completed when the sky is dark.

Here in Pondicherry, a coastal city three hours south of Chennai, pétanque is as commonplace as a mini-thali sambar-rice lunch, or the briny tang drifting out of Goubert Fish Market first thing every morning. It is integral to Pondicherry in the same way that cricket feels more Indian than British, but the sport's slower pace and quieter sounds reflect a different colonial and cultural trajectory compared to the rest of the country. Indeed, it is one of many aspects of Pondicherry life that appear completely local and foreign, unusual and traditional at the same time.

Most frequently acknowledged for its French colonial story, Pondicherry has transcended its (plural) European influences to become a city unlike any other in India. An ideal destination for the amateur historian, it is also home to centuries-old Tamil fisher families whose only reference point is the Bay of Bengal lapping at their doors. A source of antique wooden furniture for Chennaiites renovating their homes, it is a well-preserved study in Dutch, French, British and Tamil architecture. Known for the internationally recognized

Sri Aurobindo Ashram, it is also an alcohol-friendly oasis for its nearly dry neighbour state, Tamil Nadu. Indeed, Pondicherry is a post-colonial cultural melee: a series of boules being flung at each other.

Somehow, popular writing about Pondicherry does not capture these collisions. Rather, the city has been painted as a sleepy village hamlet; an ode to France; quaint: that one-syllable word with a hard ending and a seemingly soft meaning. But 'quaintness' goes deeper than its current hapless connotation. In the twelfth century, it was a French word, 'cointe', that meant 'knowledgeable, well-informed; clever; arrogant, proud; elegant, gracious'. From France, cointe swam across the Channel, where, in Middle English, it came to mean 'cunning, ingenious; proud'. This upgraded to 'elaborate, skilfully made' in the thirteenth century, and 'strange and clever' by the mid-fourteenth century. The word then resurfaced in the eighteenth century to mean 'old-fashioned but charming', which has stuck. Gone is its sharp-edged arrogance and shrewdness; today, quaint is used to imply something practically opposite in meaning. By being denied its history, this powerful word has been reduced to a whiff of nostalgia, a memory in sepia.

But Pondicherry is indeed elegant, cunning, skilfully made, strange and, yes, old-fashioned. The union territory pays tender homage to both its Tamil and French lineage, continuing to celebrate France's Bastille Day every 14 July, as well as its own liberation dates—

plural—on 16 August and 1 November. The French had arrived in Pondicherry in 1673 and, in 1714, made the mistake of banning the 'pagan feast' of Pongal, a South India-wide festival, out of respect for the foreign missionaries who had settled there. 'In protest, almost all the local population left the city. Without the Indians performing many essential tasks for the colonizers, the city could not function and this showed how limited the expression of French sovereignty was. To convince the natives to come back, the officials had to promise that such a prohibition would never again be implemented.' A little arrogant, a little gracious. A little quaint.

A little clairvoyant too: the quaintness attracted one Aurobindo Ghose and his mind-expanding principles. An unknown entity, the Bengali snuck into Pondicherry in 1910 and by 1930 had set up the Sri Aurobindo Ashram, today an iconic establishment that attracts people from all over the world. When he died in 1950, about 60,000 people—ministers, diplomats, intellectuals, spiritual leaders and the general populace—gathered for his funeral. Final rites were required to take place within forty-eight hours of death, per French law, but permission was obtained to delay Sri Aurobindo's by three days so that his devotees could assemble. Having had the wherewithal to make space for one stranger, the city opened itself up to several thousand more. Whether because of the Ashram, or those who come in search of it, Pondicherry exudes a certain calmness that makes it the envy of other cities.

Present-day circumstances, however, are less quaint—using any interpretation of that word. Pondicherry has one of the highest suicide rates in the country. Even faraway *New York Times* has discussed how badly the city's landfills are affecting the surrounding areas. Pondicherry University students went on strike in 2015, which was the same year Sri Aurobindo Ashram was under investigation for harassment. And amongst locals, issues as varied as financial debt, French visas, and environmental erosion pose long-standing challenges.

Whatever we make of Pondicherry's quaintness, one thing is certain. It has been arranging and rearranging itself ever since it was pétanqued onto a patch of South Indian land where different boules—artists, journalists, scholars, language learners, DJs, tourists, students, labourers, shop owners, ashramites—tok-tok against each other. Here in the park, tucked inside a long line of buildings and gardens that face the roaring waves, the game is on, the boules in play. Some confront each other, some keep their distance, others roll purposefully in different directions. Watch and listen carefully, for they are narrating a story that is plentiful, paradoxical, polylingual—and locating Pondicherry more precisely on the map.

ONE

Maps and Metaphors

Some of South India's most creative nomenclature comes from the city of pétanque. Although best known as Pondicherry, two thousand years ago it was Poduke, and a dozen years ago it reincarnated into Puducherry. There were several name changes in between, inevitably moving towards something less European and more Tamil, heralding a cultural, political, social revolution along the way.

I start my research in a sunny library one block south of Joan of Arc Park. Carefully folded to fit into tiny drawers are 100-, 200-, 325-year-old maps of Pondicherry. Squiggles denote rivers and fields; lines divide foreign and local populations; boxes mark homes that have been clustered by community. Opening a map is to step into a historical moment: time is measured by the yellowed paper and faded ink, space is measured by the key at the bottom left or right corner, and colonial rule is spelled in different European alphabets. Arrayed on the table, with books serving as paperweights to hold down the corners, these maps display a lively timeline.

What began as a Tamil settlement in the first century CE served as a busy trading post for the Romans, who documented the city using versions of Poduke and Puduvai. In the twelfth century, some scholars referred to it as Vedapuri: a place of Vedic knowledge. In the mid-sixteenth century, the colonial story began when the Portuguese settled there; in their records they called it Puducheira. The Dutch spent the early seventeenth century in Poelisjeri, introducing new vowels into the name. The Danes arrived twenty years later, in the 1630s, but lost the land to France twice over the next ninety years. A Dutch map produced in 1690 announced their territory as Podechery, and another map made in 1694, one year after having gained their fort back from France for the second time, used a new spelling, Poedechery. This newly added 'e' is silent by itself, but when paired with an 'o' becomes a round, audible 'oo'; perhaps symbolic of the noisy effort required to win the city back.

By this time, the Mughal emperor Aurangzeb was about thirteen years into his political campaigns in the south. One of his soldiers, Bhimsen, was also a reporter, and his memoir, *Tarikh-i-Dilkusha*, written in Persian, mentions his visit with Aurangzeb to 'Phulchery'. The French had resumed power by the time of Aurangzeb's death in 1707, and titled a map they produced in 1748 'Plan de la Ville de Pondicheri'. This introduced the nasal 'n' of the French language, and replaced the swoop of the 'y' at the end of the word with an 'i'. Could this have been visually symbolic? A play on the French word chéri, meaning darling?

With the Dutch out of the picture, the beloved settlement endured a seventy-year-long tug of war between the British and the French. A 1778 map calls the fortified city Pondichery, which could be a French or British spelling, since a key at the bottom of the map states—in French—that it was 'fait par les Anglais', or made by the British. A year later, a new map reasserted French dominance with a beret over the 'e': Pondichéry. This became a permanent fixture starting 1816, when the territory was 'finally and definitively restored to France'.

Maps through the nineteenth and twentieth centuries kept the accent on the 'e' until the French left India. From 1954 onwards, the territory became Indian and, in a country that loves its long, rolling 'r', the name grew to Pondicherry. This version gave rise to the popular nickname Pondy, which was tacked on to businesses, hotels, resorts and cafés: Le Pondy; PondyCAN; Pondy Cycle Tour, etc. Pondy is catchy, easy to say and, thanks to the city's tourism industry, still connotes clean beaches, exotic food, and charming eateries. Ask college students in Chennai what their weekend plans are, and a predictable answer is 'Pondy' and 'sarakku', as these youth go looking for alcohol-friendly escapes.

÷

3

Current maps of South India show that Pondicherry borders, and is intermingled with, the state of Tamil Nadu—itself named out of its pride for the Tamil language. From Pondicherry, the city has become a compound of two Tamil words, pudu and cheri, to make Puducherry. In fact, pudu means new, and cheri means village, so this latest name means new village— something Pondicherry might have been back in the sixteenth century, but is hardly so 500 years and several architectural resurrections later.

Today the place alternates between Puducherry and Pondicherry, just as many Indian cities ping-pong between their Indian and colonial names: Mumbai and Bombay; Chennai and Madras; Kolkata and Calcutta; Bengaluru and Bangalore. But these Tier-1 cities, established metropolitan zones with thriving commerce, culture and scholarship, boast a simple either/or nomenclature at most. It is worth noting that Puducherry, much tinier and far less conspicuous, has boasted several avatars.

While those many names evoke a turbulent, adventurous past, the present has been levelled by the Indian Census and its standardized naming schema. 'Puducherry' is the name of multiple entities nestled within each other, starting with the largest, the union territory, and working its way down to the census's smallest administrative units. In between these are mid-sized Puducherrys with government descriptors like 'metropolitan region' and 'urban agglomeration'.

For the biographer, therefore, an early question is how much of the city of Puducherry comes from its role as administrative capital of the union territory, and how much from its tourist-friendly metropolitan lifestyle.

The answer requires more maps and more history. Puducherry is one of seven union territories (UT) in India, comprising four 'districts' or 'enclaves': Mahe, Yanam, Karaikal and the eponymous Puducherry. Like some of the other UTs, it is not contiguous; its sub-territories are spread across South India, from Mahe in Kerala to Yanam in Andhra Pradesh. Karaikal and Puducherry are within the UT's borders, themselves an archipelago of settlements islanded by Tamil Nadu. These enclaves were jointly administered by the French as comptoirs, or trading settlements, for roughly 300 years until 1954. They continue as a collective entity today, although their prominence as European tourist towns has waned at different rates. There was a fifth district, located forty-five minutes north of Calcutta, called Chandannagar—formerly Chandernagore—but it quit the French dominion in 1949, six years earlier and one referendum sooner than its southern counterparts. Correspondingly, it carries a fainter presence of its colonial power.

Unlike the British departure from India, the French took eight messy years to officially hand over their comptoirs to India, marking 1954 as the de facto transfer year, and 1962 as the year the Constitution was extended to Pondicherry. But the French continue to be visible in Pondicherry through the consulate, the Alliance Française, research archives, and a certain culture and lifestyle. About 9,000 residents, or 4 per cent, are French citizens. Already unlike British India in several social and economic respects, this sets the political history of Puducherry further askew from the rest of India.

The capital of the UT is the largest enclave, also named Puducherry, with a population of about 1 million people. It is five times more populous than the next biggest enclave, and twenty times more than the smallest one. Within the capital are two municipalities: Ozhukarai in the interior and Puducherry on the east, population 250,000 (approximately) and touching the coast. But per capita density is only so illuminating. More excitingly, the eastern edge of this Puducherry boasts one of the most scenic beachfronts in the country—incidentally, it is the setting for several Bollywood movies, before more prominent Bombay and Chennai beaches are photoshopped in. So, to those unlettered in Indian Census data, and to those unfamiliar with old maps, Puducherry is neither a district nor an agglomeration, neither a colonial appendix nor a cosy village. It's a beach.

÷

As I rifled through all the names and maps of Pondicherry, the beach is the metaphor I landed on. It extends nicely: the ocean currents invited explorers to its land, and today launch fishermen to earn their livelihood. The coastal landscape inspired developers and hoteliers, and now appeals to marine biologists and divers. The horizon beckons to the borderless and the transcendentally-inclined, as it did to Aurobindo Ghose, whose spiritual centre is recognized worldwide.

Most fundamentally, perhaps, the 1.5-kilometre-long beach Promenade turns pedestrian-only from 6 p.m. to 7.30 a.m. daily, making it a walking path for locals and visitors both. People choose their tempo, strolling or striding, to make laps up and down the boulevard. Walking farther along the stretch, I turn a corner and realize that the Promenade is made up of four boulevards which form a long, unbroken oval. The eastern stretch hugs the beach, then veers right onto the southern boulevard, which meets the Railway Station and curves past the Botanical Gardens. From there the road turns into Anna Salai, parallel to the beach, before rounding onto the northern arc of the oval Sardar Vallabhai Patel Salai. One more bend in the road and I am back on the beach.

Locals refer to this area as 'within the boulevards', and this has become synonymous with 'Pondicherry' and 'home' for many whose lives and lifestyles operate inside it. The few but prominent educational outfits still run by the former colonial ruler are within the boulevards; the city has the oldest lycée, or French high school, outside of France. Enclosed in this same circle are buildings helpfully demarcated by their different coloured walls:

7

Ashram buildings are a peaceful grey, French institutions a pale yellow, and heritage French homes baby pink. They serve as complementary backdrops for the spindly bougainvillea trees and tall, old-fashioned gateways with bicycles parked outside them—which regularly inspire tourist selfies. Within these boulevards are the French patisseries, the South Indian filter coffee stalls, the North Indian jewellers, Sri Aurobindo Ashram, several temples, mosques and churches, and the myriad shops and cafés that tourists delight in.

Anna Salai is just 1.5 kilometres west of the beach; by these measurements, the area within the boulevards is a mere 8 square kilometres. But this is the heart of Pondicherry's reputation around the world. Within the boulevards are the pétanque games, handloom bazaars, yoga demonstrations, Bastille Day celebrations, jallikattu protests, and monthly salsa parties. Travellers rattle off reasons for ending up here: they seek a beach-and-nightlife scene that isn't Goa; they are interested in French history; they want to celebrate New Year's somewhere exciting, but are travelling alone, and have heard that Pondy is safe; they want to learn French and return to their hometowns in North India to join the tourism industry; their relatives from Bengal and Orissa joined Sri Aurobindo Ashram several decades ago.

But beyond the boulevards, Pondicherry thrives for equal and opposite reasons, with its own schools, temples, markets, culture, and very Tamil proper nouns. Family homes and orphanages are long-standing neighbours in Ilango Nagar, a small residential enclave where my grandparents raised eight children in the sixties and seventies. Behind it, past Saram and other neighbourhoods is the Jawaharlal Institute of Postgraduate Medical Education & Research, known countrywide as JIPMER. Veteran doctors who first trained, then practiced, and now teach at JIPMER live nearby in places like Rainbow Nagar. Those who did not go into the medical field often ended up at Tagore Arts College in Lawspet. Arikamedu is an archaeological site a few miles south of Pondicherry, where the ruins of 250-odd-year-old Spanish churches and monasteries still stand, and where millennia-old Roman coins, bricks and glass continue to be discovered today. Youth advocates and mentors from a local start-up conduct runs and bicycle rides far outside the boulevards, raising awareness about the city's alarming youth suicide rates. Important lakes and reserves are half-hour drives from the beach, well outside the oval. Pondicherry University, a central government-funded institution, sits about thirty minutes north of the northern boulevard. Next to it is the Pondicherry Engineering University, as well as one of the city's major hospitals, PIMS (Pondicherry Institute of Medical Sciences). Although less frequented by outsiders, Pondicherry, beyond the boulevards, is just as bustling.

9

A strip of beach, an oval of streets, a union of territories, a monologue of maps, a Franco-Tamoul culture. Within and without the boulevards, Pondicherry coexists in its many forms. And to capture each of them, this city biography, with its metaphors and characters, must use a kind of storytelling that is part fact, part flânerie, part folklore. In a city where Hindu sages and French oracles are buried under the earth, we must consider how the landscape came to be in the first place.

TWO

A Landscape of Portraits

Gazing far, far above the earth, where maps make little sense, astronomers have long pondered the epic distances between stars, planets, and moons. Guillaume-Joseph-Hyacinthe-Jean-Baptiste Le Gentil was one such reader of the skies, whose enthusiasm took him from France to the Indian Ocean in 1761 to observe the 'Transit of Venus', a rare sighting of the planet's orbit set against the backdrop of the sun. What Le Gentil envisioned as a trip to Pondicherry for a singular purpose became a serpentine eleven-year journey to the East.

Studying various longitudes and latitudes while sailing to India, the Frenchman noted that 'geography owes its actual perfection to the progress which astronomy has made during the last fifty years, and for that reason astronomers must be regarded as the true geographers'. But for all his precision and measurements, Gentil's chosen science could not control the political winds blowing about India's colonies—the mid-eighteenth century was witnessing a violent back and forth between Pondicherry's French and British rulers. When his ship docked on the subcontinent's southwestern coast, just a few days shy of Pondicherry, Le Gentil and the crew 'learned from the ships of this country that this place was in the possession of the English, and that Pondicherry no longer existed for us'.

The ship was redirected to the Isle de France— now Mauritius—where Le Gentil's ability to observe Venus was much diminished. He spent the next five years exploring Mauritius and Madagascar 'to make all the observations that I could on geography, natural history, physics, astronomy, navigation, winds, and tides'. Keeping busy thus 'compensated me to some extent and made me wait for the transit of Venus in 1769, the sole and last transit that the present generation could hope to see'.

In 1766, Le Gentil calculated that the best location for this sighting was Manila, Philippines. After securing the necessary approvals from ship captains and governments, he set sail from Isle de France on 1 May 1766, 'quite resolved to say good-bye forever to that island' and ultimately return to France via east Asia and the Americas. But due to more political instability, he reached Manila and was told that he could not stay. Hearing that Pondicherry was back under French rule again, Le Gentil fled the Philippines on another ship, this time headed west. He reached Pondicherry in 1768 and was received warmly by Governor General Law de Lauriston. This was the welcome Le Gentil had hoped for seven years earlier, and he now enthusiastically set about building an observatory on the ruins of a former governor's palace, since destroyed by the British, but not completely. 'All this excellent masonry of brick, of limestone, and of sand, had resisted the effects of the gunpowder and was quite whole and quite solid; but the pavilions were partly fallen. I went to visit the remains of these pavilions; I looked at the most easterly', which was closest to the beach. With approval from the governor, and collaborating with the chief engineer, Le Gentil had his observatory installed there.

Finally on solid ground, among fellow Frenchmen, with an actual observatory full of all the equipment he had painstakingly brought over from France, Le Gentil was ready to work, and to wait. 'I enjoyed at Pondicherry that sweet peace which is the support of muses; I occupied myself in the midst of this peace in devoting happy moments to Uranus; with my soul content and satisfied I await with such tranquillity until the approaching ecliptic conjunction of Venus with the sun comes to terminate my academic courses.'

When 3 June 1769 arrived, Le Gentil was fully prepared. But he was thwarted once again. Cloud cover rolled in, as uncontrollable as colonial battles and sea storms, political favour and trade winds. 'That is the fate which often awaits astronomers,' Le Gentil mourned. 'I had gone more than ten thousand leagues; it seemed that I had crossed such a great expanse of seas, exiling myself from my native land, only to be the spectator of a fatal cloud which came to place itself before the sun at the precise moment of my observation, to carry off

13

from me the fruits of my pains and of my fatigues...'

Le Gentil was defeated. Not surprisingly, he was now in a hurry to return home. But illness delayed him and bad weather forced ships to reroute via the Isle de France more than once. By the time he arrived home in 1771 he had been presumed dead; his family was even quarrelling over his assets.

Pondicherry, however, has memorialized him differently. Where his observatory once stood on the city's beach Promenade is a 30-metre-tall lighthouse. Symbolically studying the skies, forecasting the weather, and reassuring ships on the horizon that they will reach safely, it is an apt reminder of the French astronomer's adventures and misadventures in Pondicherry. And a premonition of the explorers to come—via the sea, the air, or on foot.

÷

Built in 1836, the lighthouse is one of several constructions that line the city's beach. In fact, the beachscape tells its own story of Pondicherry's history and geography—and astronomy—and walking up and down the beach Promenade becomes the equivalent of listening to the city's lore. Although perfectly straight and ideal for brisk walking routines, the Promenade is more nomadic than it looks. The building signage announces private, government, and historical sites, drawing some walkers away from their laps to investigate further. And the tides of people who crowd the Promenade, whether for a morning walk, an evening stroll, or something in between, are themselves a study in diversity, choreography and anthropology.

Charles Baudelaire, French poet and essayist of the mid-nineteenth century, first wrote about the Parisian flâneur in his essay 'The Painter of Modern Life'—a curious breed of observer for whom 'The crowd is his element, as the air is that of birds and water of fishes. His passion and his profession are to become one flesh with the crowd. For the perfect *flâneur*, for the passionate spectator, it is an immense joy to set up house in the heart of the multitude, amid the ebb and flow of movement, in the midst of the fugitive and the infinite.'

With perked ears and piqued curiosity, the flâneur is alert to the changes around him: distinct faces on the streets; new fashion trends; the quality of the sunlight on a summer day versus a winter evening. In twenty-first-century Pondicherry, as in nineteenth-century Paris, observations must begin in the morning—in fact, before the morning—for if the flâneur 'opens his eyes to see the boisterous sun beating a tattoo upon his window-pane, he reproaches himself remorsefully and regretfully: "What a peremptory order! what a bugle-blast of life! Already several hours of light—everywhere—lost by my sleep! How many *illuminated* things might I have seen and have missed seeing!"'

Dawn in Pondicherry is greyish, sleepy. And it begins with a wind that blows inland from the sea.

The first structures it encounters are the statues on the beach: Gandhi's, in mid-stride; Nehru's, a few metres away, locked in a permanent staring contest with his colleague; Joan of Arc with her back to the water; and Governor Dupleix's likeness, papers in one arm, the other hand pointing downwards as if in accusation.

Further inland, daytime on Pondicherry's Promenade reveals a landscape of portraits. They are impassive stone buildings; maternal church idols; freshly whitewashed hotels; moustachioed ice-cream vendors; a lighthouse that has been dark for over forty years. Some have distinctly European features, while others resemble Bourbon Street in New Orleans. Bougainvillea trees suggest a Latin influence, but the autorickshaws, darting like bumblebees between them, ensure an Indian finish. Kolams, scrawled like signatures in front of gates, show off a distinctly South Indian calligraphy. This portraiture has hybrid, tribrid origins.

The accompanying captions are doubly, triply faithful. Architecture is Franco-Pondichérien, cuisine is Indo-Chinese. People have Christian prénoms and Hindu family names, and hotels have multilingual names like Maison Perumal. The street name Des Bassyins De Richemont Street is spelt inconsistently on official documents, and is more commonly known as 'Gujju Street'. Signs are in English, French and Tamil. The Tourism Office, which used to be in the middle of the Promenade has two clocks, one to show the time in Pondicherry and the other to keep pace with Paris.

Archive house diaries written in Tamil and drainage system blueprints in Dutch. Sri Aurobindo Ashram is named after the Bengali thinker; in Tamil, his name is spelled 'Aravindar', erasing the Bengali 'o' altogether.

The city's proper nouns insist on being memorable. 'Knowledge' is the building where Sri Aurobindo Ashram school graduates pursue higher studies. 'Heritage' can refer to one of many charming French buildings, renovated and expanded into boutique hotels, and wearing golden 'Vieilles Maisons Françaises' signs at the entrance. For its uniquely large and rare collection of Sanskrit and Tamil palm-leaf scrolls, the French Institute of Pondicherry is a registered UNESCO 'Memory of the World' site. Literally and figuratively, the city centre is bounded by knowledge, heritage, and memory.

17

Morning has arrived and the Promenade has been filling with people all the while: couples holding hands for pre-wedding photo shoots, camera crew in tow; early risers responding to the succession of calls to prayer and temple chants, marching up and down the Promenade for good vibrations; weathered ashramites setting their meditations to rhythm; and ambitious tourists taking it all in.

÷

Bass is up before 5 a.m. every day, but has no time for a morning walk. He is a butcher who must have all his meat cut, packaged and distributed to various bars and biryani stores around Pondicherry by noon.

His cubicle in Goubert Market, about ten minutes from the Promenade, is flanked by other butcher stalls, and there is a uniformity to how they are decorated, and how they display their meat. All the stalls have photos of idols and religious calendars hanging on bare nails—Hindu, Muslim, Christian; Sri Aurobindo's face is among these.

'We cut the heads open for brain fry. It's a delicacy,' Bass says, eager to show someone around; how often do tourists visit the market? He beckons to an empty stall where there is enough space to plonk down some furniture—a one-armed plastic chair and a small plastic stool. He offers me the chair and crouches on the stool. His muscles, nearly black in the dim light, bulge out of his short-sleeved polo shirt, his legs are comfortable in sweatpants. The perimeter of the cubicle is lined with cases. What are they? 'Enna case?' he repeats in Tamil, to confirm the question. 'Beer case.'

Bass is full of restless energy, fidgeting, and leaning forward on his stool. He happily answers questions about his past, which include serving a fourteen-year jail sentence for murder. He's still part of the gang he was with before his incarceration, but now feels like he is given more respect, having done time. He pronounces his name 'boss' and suggests that I do, too. Cops are the worst members of society, he warns in the same breath. Gangs should settle disputes among themselves. But Lieutenant Governor Kiran Bedi—he pronounces her first name 'Crane'—is a 'great lady', he says, his respect genuine.

18

Having lost his freedom once before, Bass lives simply and in the moment. After work, he meets his friends for languorous food-and-drink sessions. He has observed Pondicherry grow over the years, and is unhappy with how congested and unsafe it has become—something not immediately apparent during an early morning walk. While he does not have a solution for the traffic, this gangster surrounded by cases of beer does have an idea to increase safety: close the bars earlier at night so that people are less drunk and start fewer fights.

He flashes bright white teeth when he smiles, and peppers his conversation with invitations to meet later that night for biryani, or for a drink, or both. When I take up his offer some evenings later, Bass is sporting a totally different look: jeans and a leather jacket. He leads the way to a rooftop bar he particularly enjoys. 'Even vegetarians like you must drink,' he reasons. Butcher by day and convict by past, he is just one more protagonist, one more narrator, on Pondicherry's storyscaped coastline.

The sun sinks below the horizon and Pondicherry twinkles under the light. Bass raises a toast to the evening ahead. He will be at work hours before the others at the table have even woken up, but that is no reason to not enjoy beer and conversation tonight.

÷

By 7.30 a.m. every morning, the beach road is noisy with the vehicles that have replaced the walkers. Where Baudelaire's protagonist might have climbed aboard a pousse-pousse (an earlier version of the rickshaw) to convey him to his next appointment, the contemporary Pondicherry flâneur, or flâneuse, hops onto a two-wheeler—that most ubiquitous sight on Pondicherry's narrow streets. These can dart through traffic, catch the sea breeze on the Promenade, and enable frequent stops to study historical artefacts still scattered around the city. But many men on bikes seem to have no purpose besides speeding past women while whistling at them. Amusing at first, this becomes grating when it happens throughout the day, no matter the time or street, and has proven to be dangerous at night—making me think twice before setting out alone after dinner, having been not just touched, but slapped on the back, by a brazen motorist.

M. Yuvaraj, however, is a professional and experienced tourism officer, and on the back of his motorcycle it takes us only twenty minutes to complete one round of the boulevards. This includes stops to read the plaques marking the gates into Fort Louis, which was built by Governors François Martin and Joseph François Dupleix in the early eighteenth century—one of Pondicherry's most significant architectural chapters, and harbingers of today's thoroughfares and boulevards. New Madras Gate faces north, in the direction of Madras. Facing west, away from the water, is the Vazhudavur Gate—

which leads to the eponymous Tamil Nadu town of Vazhudavur. Farther southwest is Villiyanur Gate, also at the end of one of the city's main streets. This is not a coincidence. Before these streets were thoroughfares they were the only access points into and out of the fort, making them well-trodden roads when the fort existed.

Shrouded by clusters of plants, traffic signals, lamp posts, and their accompanying tangles of wires, the Fort Louis plaques are easy to miss. They look steel- or aluminium-plated, but have lost their sheen. The lettering is faded and scratched in parts, but spells out the history of the fort and the significance of each gate. Illustrations are included, as if these are pages out of a textbook. Yuvaraj sighs as he reads from the signs, ignoring the honking and engine revs around him. If only these pieces of history were respected for the knowledge and heritage they contain, he muses, a rare frown on his face. He can identify the plaques easily, having made the rounds several times, but this makes him one of few experts; the French history most tourists seek are stylish sandwiches, boutique apparel, and movie screenings at the Alliance Française. Traffic— two-, three- and four-wheeler; two-, and four-legged; purposeful and passive, all oblivious—congeals and flows without any time for introspection into an urban history.

Yuvaraj's motorcycle tour ends opposite Pondicherry's Railway Station at the final gate, Porte de Goudelour, almost hidden behind a sugarcane-crusher-

and-juice stall. Inaugurated in October 1879, this was once a tiny station whose trains shuttled only between Pondicherry and Villipuram. Today it is a crowded junction, and its trains run all the way to Calcutta, some 1,850 kilometres northeast.

÷

Aside from the oval of boulevards, Pondicherry's layout is a neat grid, all straight lines and right angles. Its various religious and ethnic communities have their own sub-grid. Phrases that sound 'quaint' in twenty-first-century India—'the French Quarter', 'the Tamil Quarter', 'the Muslim Quarter'—bring tourists into town to behold what a 'quarter' might actually look like, and how the street names change from Rue La Bourdonnais to Rue Kamatchi Amman Kovil to Rue Mullah. The French Quarter is regularly referred to as 'White Town', or 'La Ville Blanche' in French, and spans two waterways: the beach on the east, and the canal on the west, although the latter is now a dried-up channel where leaves and litter collect. Farther inland, on the other side of the canal is the quarter that people hesitate to call by its old name, 'Black Town', for obvious reasons, but the visual differences can't be denied. The streets are narrower, dirtier and more crowded; fewer street sweepers and garbage collectors can be spotted throughout the day; more signs are in Tamil than English or French and plot sizes are smaller, accommodating modern Tamil residences and shops instead of colonnaded French homes. Istriwallahs and walis—the men and women who iron clothes on street corners—know to charge the occasional vellakaaran (white person) more for their shirts. But Black Town isn't completely exempt of colonial influence. In fact, some of the oldest Catholic churches and historical institutions are located there, looming high above their local neighbours.

The historian Jean Deloche asserts that it was the Dutch who first imposed straight lines and segregated districts onto the town, back in the 1610s. Their navy, soldiers and godowns stood closer to the Bay of Bengal, surrounded by the residences of 'Malabars and Christians', and centred around a fortified area (with Danish origins) with four towers, a church, wells, and warehouses. Behind them were more rows of buildings and residences, categorized by occupation, from blacksmiths to shepherds, laundrymen to whores. These were arranged like squares on a chess board, and movement between them would have been similarly strategic. Such a layout contained the priestly class of Brahmins to one sector, 'Chettis' (or Chettiyars, the merchant caste) to another, and 'Komuttis' (or Komatis, the money lenders) to yet another.

When Captain François Martin and his army took control of Pondicherry in 1674, they retained the compartmentalized system. Still, they needed an area for themselves, from which they could rule over the entire trading port, with one eye on the beachfront, keeping

23

a lookout for visitors, and another on the hinterland where the locals bartered goods and gossip in their bazaars. Taking his cues from the Danes and then the Dutch, Martin began constructing a high-walled 'fort oblong', a trapezoidal fort buttressed by five towers and gates. Within it, the French army kept watch, conducted business, ran the government, oversaw trade, and supervised their factories.

Governor Dupleix arrived in 1742 and christened it Fort Louis. He refined its shape into a perfect pentagon that he dreamed would become a palace worthy of any French king. While conducting a walking tour of Pondicherry—yet another form of flânerie—a researcher at INTACH (Indian National Trust for Art and Cultural Heritage) pointed out that the width of Pondicherry's Promenade was the thickness of Governor Dupleix's fort wall. More than 250 years later, what was once impenetrable stone is now a breezy, beachy Promenade; what was once a stony ruin has become a lighthouse.

÷

Over fifty-odd years, the French and the British did their best to upset the other's way of life in Pondicherry during their many land disputes. In 1761, the English razed the French fort and churches which, the French, when they regained control four years later, painstakingly reconstructed. This happened again in 1816 when the British left Pondicherry for the last time. Churches in the city's French Quarter wear plaques with several dates: a version of L'Eglise de Notre Dame des Anges has been built four times, copying different models, for example. Noteworthy here is that in spite of so many periods of reconstruction, the streets have remained at right angles; the quarters on either side of the canal. If one unfolds and stacks all those ancient maps of Pondicherry on top of each other, the changes are incremental, showing a settlement that grew out of a coastal trading post into a gridded town indexed by profession, enhanced with smart waterways and navigable streets, decorated with church spires and fort towers and a financial centre with a Dutch and then French coin mint. Although the fort no longer exists—save the plaques on the boulevards— and the churches now keep company with temples and mosques, the canal still runs north–south, and the streets are still a grid.

25

But some of Pondicherry's most important spaces are circles, not squares. Starting in the centre of the town is Bharati (also spelled Bharathi) Park—a beautiful space, green and peaceful, ideal for children, walkers, families and couples. Outside the park, streets emanate like spokes. They meet the rest of the street grid at odd angles, creating cosy boundaries on the road for a badminton match on a sleepy, traffic-free morning. On these streets are a range of buildings. The decrepit 'Puducherry Archives' office is a single dusty room laden with old *Gazettes*; Cercle de Pondicherry athletic club, franchises of which existed in Saigon and Hanoi, is large, glossy-white and clinging onto its still-exclusive membership. Raj Nivas, or Government House, is where the current Lieutenant Governor resides; it has been rebuilt several times as well, back when the British and the French claimed that space for their reigning governor. Policemen stand at attention at the imposing gates, recognizable by their red hats, also called 'kepis'.

From the park one can spot bookshops announcing massive sales in bold letters, or walk over to deposit a check at UCO Bank. Or one can wait while loved ones are treated at the General Hospital (GH) across the street. A good way to pass the time is to enjoy fresh coconut water from Sengeni amma who is permanently stationed in the southwest corner of the circle just outside the park.

÷

Having taken all this in, the flâneur rushes to his desk, 'darting on to a sheet of paper the same glance that a moment ago he was directing towards external things, skirmishing with his pencil, his pen, his brush, splashing his glass of water up to the ceiling, wiping his pen on his shirt, in a ferment of violent activity, as though afraid that the image might escape him...' Whether or not I manage to achieve this, 'the external world is reborn' for Baudelaire's documentarian, 'natural and more than natural, beautiful and more than beautiful, strange and endowed with an impulsive life like the soul of its creator. The phantasmagoria has been distilled from nature. All the raw materials with which the memory has loaded itself are put in order, ranged and harmonized, and undergo that forced idealization which is the result of a childlike perceptiveness—that is to say, a perceptiveness acute and magical by reason of its innocence!'

THREE

Water from a Whore

Peter Heehs, a historian, poet and dramatist, likes to jog in the morning. He starts on the beach but ends in Bharati Park where the crowd isn't so thick. Turning at the Old Lighthouse, he crosses the Gandhi Thidal— Tamil for plaza—and enters the park through the one gate that is unlocked. 'There didn't use to be gates here,' he remembers, his slow American accent nearly a drawl. 'Not even walls. You could just cross the park as you were walking from one part of town to another.'

Temple bells sound from a few feet away and Heehs tells me their story with a chuckle: 'The murti of that temple was one of these pieces of sculpture that came possibly from Gingee or somewhere else. One fine day, a Brahmin attached himself to it and became its custodian. Gradually, he began doing puja there, and gradually it grew, and a piece of sculpture slowly became a living temple. And now it looks like it's been there forever.'

Bharati Park is a museum of such stories, and its curators include Heehs, who has lived in Pondicherry for over forty years, young lovers seeking privacy, and uniform-wearing schoolchildren scaling the park's artificial mountains. Pieces of the sixteenth-century Gingee Fort ruins dot the park, extracted from their original location 75 kilometres northwest and installed by the French; today they are anachronistic, totem pole-like adornments found in between curls of trees. Equally figurine-like are the pink-jacketed city cleaners hunched over the soil, composting the park's waste.

Heehs and his morning colleagues follow walking paths that draw geometric patterns inside the park. These converge at a monument in the centre of the park: tall, white, and pillared. Unlike the grainy stone of the Gingee sculptures, this monument is the kind of immaculate white stone that evokes Western architecture. Its pillars and triangular roof make it European, and the tall fleur-de-lis positioned on the dome above the roof marks it as French, and proudly so.

Inside the monument, one might expect to see a statue, given that the rest of Pondicherry is full of them. But there is nothing besides a dry stone basin that used to hold a 'large fountain', as labelled on a map from 1891. Two granite-plated stones at the base of the monument bear inscriptions—but one is in Latin and the other in Tamil, which leaves me even more perplexed about what the monument represents. Could it be a gift from the Portuguese Jesuit priests who needed to build an altar when they first arrived in the early sixteenth century? The homesick French who wanted to erect reminders of Paris in their new colony?

Ask a local, and they will tell you that it's the Aayi Mandapam. But few can tell you who, or what, Aayi is. Or why its architecture is Greco-Roman and why its description, mandapam, is the Tamil word for hall.

The mystery of Aayi is a 500-year-old story that starts with a Deccan king and ends with a French emperor. Included in the cast are an agriculturalist with 'a physiological peculiarity—a thick growth of hair on his soles', a 'femme de joie' (harlot), and a nineteenth-century chief engineer of Paris.

These descriptions come from *A Concise History of Pondicherry*, written by P. Raja, a self-described 'fifth generation' Pondicherrian, bilingual writer and retired professor of English literature. He has written several books about his hometown, and celebrated the story of Aayi more than once. He even converted the myth into a play called *Water Please* and published it in 2014. Having given this odd array of characters a stage, Raja sets them all against the backdrop of a prediction made by Pavazhakodi Siddha, an enlightened saint whose tantric powers allowed him to live for hundreds of years.

Two modern-day characters in *Water Please* are overheard recounting the water problems that Pondicherry faced in the 1800s, from severe shortages endured by the French, to the undrinkable condition of the water when it was finally available. One character recalls what the wise siddha had foretold about how potable water would eventually come to Pondicherry.

As Raja writes:

> The Siddha meditated awhile and then said
> without opening his eyes: '...A curse has fallen
> on the White Town dwellers. The cure will come
> with a Whiteman and they are destined to have
> water from a whore.'

Unlike *Mughal-e-Azam* and other well-worn tales of
courts and courtesans, this Deccan yarn has a crucial
foreign participant—the 'Whiteman'—and unspools
from Telugu into French, Tamil, and Latin. Like any
story, this one is best told by starting at the beginning.

÷

Once upon a time there lived a king. His name
was Krishnadeva Raya and he was the ruler of the
Vijayanagara empire, which spread from the southern tip
of India and covered about one-fifth of the subcontinent,
reaching as far north as present-day Karnataka, and
nearly touching the Maharashtra border. During one of
his many travels through his kingdom, the king took a
detour through the town of Villianur in order to meet
a Mudaliar whose reputation preceded him: he was a
nobleman who wore sandals of gold.

But Krishnadeva Raya stumbled upon an even
more wondrous sight that made him forget all about
the glittering footwear he had pilgrimaged so far
for. Somewhere near his destination stood a building
so ornate and luminescent that he knew, as only a

discerning king could, that it was a sacred temple. All kings are knelt before, but great ones can kneel as well, when the occasion demands it. And Krishnadeva Raya fell to his knees before the massive structure and meditated, his entourage following suit.

The king could feel a divine silence pressing on his head as he bowed down, as if acknowledging his prayers. But the pressure grew palpable, more a strain than a blessing. The king opened his eyes to see villagers gathered around him, wearing flustered expressions on their faces. He stood up—a king did not prostrate before his people—and glared back, until one daring villager stepped forward and asked why His Majesty was bent over before *this* place, of all places.

Because it reminds me of the humility of man in the face of spiritual supremacy, the king said.

The villager hesitated.

The king demanded an explanation. How dare this commoner question him!

The villager looked up at the mansion, then back at the king. Did His Majesty know what lay within its walls?

The king turned to his adviser, whose gestures were unreadable. The king turned back. Wasn't there a deity inside this sanctum? Something beautiful, unattainable, irresistible, and ever benevolent?

The villager's face turned red. Yes, there was someone inside. Yes, she was beautiful and unattainable. But not by divine grace. No, she was a temple dancer regularly patronized by the wealthy men of the village, a Devadasi whose livelihood came from charm and beauty, a woman who was craved by every man in His Majesty's empire.

The king could not believe what he was hearing. He demanded that the whore be called outside and made to answer for her grotesque behaviour. To think he had almost considered replicating the property's proportions as an addition to his own palace!

A woman appeared at the gate and the king nearly fell to his knees again. Never before had he seen someone so arresting, with eyes like the tips of a javelin, collar bones with a heart-shaped hollow at the centre, a torso that curved around wholesome hips. As she surveyed the crowd, her slight movements made music out of her bangles, her necklaces danced against her breasts, and her anklets tinkled, filling him with lust.

But the king held himself steady and began firing questions at her before she could say anything; he feared that her voice would cause his knees to buckle.

Who was she, and what possessed her to live in such a palatial home? Did she not know the difference between humans and gods; did she think she could dress her house up as a place of worship and fool her master of masters? Did women in her trade confuse themselves for apsaras who could extract whatever they chose from the mortal men they seduced? Did she think of no one but herself, in living so gaudily?

The woman stood erect, unfazed. Aayi, she said,

answering his first question. Her name was Aayi.

Even as she pronounced these two syllables the king could feel his head spinning. His harem was full, but he had to find a way to take her back with him. He would rebuild this very palace on his grounds where she could live in luxury and attend to him whenever he desired.

Of course, he did not say this out loud. Grapes that are out of reach become sour, and so did Aayi's magnificent home.

Destroy it, he heard himself say. No one must covet this home or what it stands for. In its place, build something that quenches human yearning. Create something that will last forever—far longer than the feminine tinsel that beguiles mankind so. He loudly announced that he would forgive her if she carried out his orders.

Aayi knew better than to disagree with a king, particularly when he was embarrassed. It was her turn to yield, her back to her house, her head bowed before the king.

I know what to do, Your Majesty, she whispered. The king's heart leapt; it was as if they were having a private conversation, as if she belonged only to him. And then, so that she could be heard by everyone: You want something that quenches, so I will build a well. You want something that lasts forever, so I will build a tank. Its water will be the purest in all of Vijayanagara, and will be memorialized as Your Majesty's lesson for

34

a lowly mortal whose ego was bigger than her home.

King Krishnadeva Raya smiled to hide his misery. As far as the people could see, she was obeying orders; to him she was sweetly, pointedly identifying his hubris. She is more cunning than my best ministers, the king thought. But after the way I have behaved, I can only banish her from this place, not invite her into my court.

With a nod and a swish of his hand, the king agreed to Aayi's idea and climbed back onto his horse. The royal retinue galloped off into the night. King Krishnadeva Raya's adviser knew, from the way his master urged his horse onward, faster, farther from the village, that he was trying to outrun his own shame. They never spoke of the incident.

Meanwhile, Aayi's house was razed to the ground with the same festivity with which it had been constructed, for Aayi was a woman full of love, music and laughter. Aayikulam, as the tank was named, sparkled with the life of its creator.

Three hundred years after Krishnadeva Raya's reign, the French had settled in Pondicherry, but were struggling to procure clean water. Despite the Dutch canals and drainage systems and all the wells that had been dug, the water in the French Quarter, closest to the sea, was undrinkable. A desperate Monsieur Bontemps, Governor of Pondicherry from 1863 to 1871, wrote to Paris for help, and Napoleon III dispatched Chief Engineer Lamairesse halfway across the world to devise a sustainable fix.

35

It took Monsieur Lamairesse a few months to study the water in different parts of Pondicherry from White Town to Black Town. He went beyond the boulevards to locate as many water sources as he could, and ultimately found Aayi's legacy, still beautiful, still irresistible, ever benevolent. He constructed channels and a pulley system to bring water from Aayi's tank less than 10 kilometres east to a well he dug in the centre of town. He was so moved by the story of Aayi that he wrote to Napoleon about it. The emperor responded with a clear instruction to Bontemps: 'Be grateful to Aayi. She deserves a monument.' He commissioned the mandapam to be built on top of the well, so that the structure stood majestically at the centre of Pondicherry's Government Square. Constructed in 1854, it remained singularly conspicuous for at least fifty years, and today marks the centre of Bharati Park.

About 50 metres in front of the enigmatic mandapam is a much more colourful, self-explanatory statue: a smiling woman dressed in a sari pours water out of a pot.

÷

Asking Pondicherrians of varying vintage about Aayi Mandapam produces inconsistent results. History aficionados know the story of King Krishnadeva Raya and the Devadasi. Some have even read about Aayi's three sisters—Oosi, Bangari and Singari—all Devadasis who left behind legacies in the form of tanks, canals, wells and lakes. Many locals have visited Oosi's namesake, a lake named Ousteri, also called Ossudu, for picnics and boat rides. Siva Mathiyazhagan knows that the mandapam is also the official emblem of the union territory; he uses it on banners advertising his youth advocacy organization, Trust for Youth and Child Leadership. My father recalled the rumours that his school friends had spread about a secret sorangam, or tunnel, that went all the way from Aayi Mandapam to Gingee Fort, 75 kilometres northwest. He was not entirely wrong: there was once a tunnel that began under the Gandhi statue on Beach Road to be built upto Gingee Fort. It was terminated after workers died during its construction and roads began caving in.

Heehs points to the pieces of the 500-year-old sculptures positioned on his walking path: 'The French liked them, so they brought them here,' he says, a slight edge to his voice. 'Some of them have ended up in that temple in the corner of the park, and now people pray to them.'

Perhaps this is the visual for Pondicherry: a monument that few people know about is at the centre of a park, erected with great pomp by the French and, unusually, dedicated to a Tamil danseuse—while nearby stands a Hindu temple that came up out of thin air, and is faithfully visited throughout the day by locals of all ages. In both cases the origin story is unknown; the deity is an abstraction; the inspiration is Tamil folklore; and both live in Bharati Park—and the two visuals could not be more unlike each other.

Chief Engineer Lamairesse ensured that the tank supplied fresh water to the city for some two hundred years—long before French architect Le Corbusier organized post-Independence Chandigarh or American architects designed Durgapur in West Bengal. Yuvaraj points me to the website of Puducherry Agro Service and Industries Corporation (PASIC), which claims to have been bottling and marketing natural mineral water from a local source, and supplying 'Pondichéry Water' to the Rashtrapati Bhavan as well as embassies and consulates in New Delhi since 1989. The website has not been updated since 2014, but the story does resonate with Aayi and her powers.

Sadly, Aayikulam has dried up, and today the union territory of Pondicherry faces water shortages like its neighbours Tamil Nadu and Karnataka, all of whom receive water from the Kaveri River. This has gravely affected Karaikal district, where farmers depend heavily on the river for irrigation. Pondicherry's Department of Agriculture states that about 45 per cent of the union territory is involved in agriculture 'directly or indirectly', but that the sector contributes less than 2 per cent of the Gross State Domestic Product (GSDP).

This imbalance is seen in other aspects of the annual budget. Being a union territory, Pondicherry is centrally funded. The *Times of India* reported that Pondicherry ranked fourth in per capita income in 2016—but also has very high per capita debt. Through the Swadesh

38

Darshan scheme, a central government fund promoting 'theme based tourist circuits', the union territory was granted over ₹100 crore in 2017 to develop its heritage and spiritual tourism. Central and local governments agree that this is the industry to focus on, but the supporting infrastructure—roads and traffic, sewage and garbage disposal systems, clean waterways—needs to become more robust. It is currently sagging under the local growth and urbanization taking place. Still, Lieutenant Governor Kiran Bedi has been organizing clean-up efforts on the canal during her tenure, and has included it as a specific item in the Swadesh Darshan scheme.

A UN-sponsored 'Pondicherry Vision 2020' report is optimistic about the union territory's service sector, thanks to its 'good educational infrastructure and human development base', which is explored in later chapters. The IT and communication sectors show strong potential—which Pondicherry should act on by 'upgrading services such as transport, housing and banking'.

The city is perceptive; it acknowledges that its streets are filling up. For every new unavailable parking spot, there is another entrepreneur tapping into the city's creative energy, laid-back pace of life, and general open-mindedness, launching a sound engineering and acoustics business, a solar-panelling service, or a vegan café whose employees are newly empowered village women. Indians settled abroad are buying properties on the beach, driving rates up as they establish their vacation residences. Young couples are moving from North India to breathe cleaner air and enrol their children in the Ashram school. At the same time, many local youngsters are leaving to work in bigger cities like Chennai, Bangalore and Hyderabad. Still, the Promenade swells each evening with new faces moving at new clips, thinking about new ways to be a part of Pondicherry's new economy. I wonder: do the siddhas have new prophecies about where the city's water—and commerce, and industry—will come from?

Because it *did* happen that a siddha's transcendental words came true, and that Pondicherrians followed their destiny to drink 'water from a whore'. A French emperor's gratitude was commissioned on the ashes of an Indian emperor's chagrin. And a Devadasi named Aayi dances invisibly around Bharati Park, attracting morning walkers and evening playground climbers into her flowing embrace.

40

FOUR

Namma Bhaashai

If the tale of Aayi Mandapam was ever to be made into a movie, the perfect man for the job could be found a few streets away, sitting on the rooftop of Rathna Theatre. Thribhuvan Vijay Manoharan's family started and own the single-screen theatre that is a city landmark. Whether in a thick beard and lungi, as if preparing for a pilgrimage, or clean-shaven in a button-down shirt and looking years younger, Thribhuvan moves around Pondicherry like the local he is: on his motorcycle, bright-eyed, observant, and constantly puzzling over the next great script to be written.

Rathna Theatre—originally Rathna Talkies—belonged to Thribhuvan's great-grandfather, and was first a 'touring talkie', a mobile projector that travelled around the region. It was the French who gave the theatre a plot of land to permanently set up in; Thribhuvan's relatives recall that people from nearby villages would travel by bullock cart to Pondicherry to watch movies. But Thribhuvan is fuzzy on the exact details—dates, legalities—and prefers to call his family history a kind of folklore. 'Ippadi thaan solranga,' the thirty-odd-year-old says, quoting his father, who begins all Rathna-related stories with this disclaimer in Tamil: 'This is how they tell it.'

As Thribhuvan tells it, Rathna Theatre is a nearly seventy-year-old family legacy. The building's structure and skeleton reflect its age: the cement floor inside the movie hall is only partially carpeted and the seats rise at a gentler-than-usual incline. The building is wide, with a U-shaped driveway in the front for customers to drive in, park, and later drive out. A high wall on the main road obscures the entrance into the theatre, but pedestrians can see a simple billboard fixed near the roof of the building, facing the boulevard on which the theatre sits, announcing its name in English and Tamil. Thribhuvan wants to light it up, 'like on Broadway'. Next to it, he plans to instal one of the old movie projectors in homage to Rathna's past. 'If you ask me why it's called Rathna Theatre, only my great-grandfather knows...it was probably the name of his first love!'

Thribhuvan has a flair for melodrama. Growing up in Pondicherry and working in the film industry in Chennai, he switches naturally between Tamil and English, peppering his storytelling with movie and actor references. He learned French in school, but points out that the subject was taught as theory, not as a skill. 'I can write an essay without a grammar mistake, but I can't talk about the same topic.' His history lesson about French rule in Pondicherry was 'just a half page or page of a text book: It was a French colony, there were some wars, and then there was a transition between one government and another.' And when history comes to life in Pondicherry, such as on France's National Day, Thribhuvan is clear about who participates. 'The *people* don't celebrate Bastille Day. The *French* celebrate it here.'

Indeed, the city's French culture feels miles away from this institution on the western boulevard. And Thribhuvan's version of its history comes from his theatre, not from textbooks. He dates changes in the city, and in his theatre, based on the movies they were screening at the time. The sound system, he remembers, was upgraded before the screening of *Titanic*, and moviegoers could feel the old iron pillars vibrating as the ship began its slow collapse. (I later confirm that the digital technology Rathna switched to became available in 1997, the same year as James Cameron's epic.)

43

Titanic was one of the many English movies that Rathna Talkies screened. In fact, Rathna stayed competitive by sticking to English movies for decades. 'When other theatres came in, we allowed them to take over Tamil, and we catered to the Ashram and foreign crowd in Pondicherry.' Then a JIPMER medical student, Mr Balakrishnan remembers taking his fiancée there on a date in the late sixties, to see *A Fistful of Dollars* starring Clint Eastwood. Locals who knew only Tamil would come too, eager to see a foreign film, so the Rathna staff would publish a movie summary in front of the main doors, in Tamil, which customers could read before the movie began since there were no subtitles. 'People would buy a ticket, stand and read the entire story, and then go inside and watch the movie,' Thribhuvan says, smiling. 'That was the golden age for us: people came for a love of cinema.'

But Rathna's English-only specialty ended in the early 2000s. Movies such as *Speed* (1994), *Anaconda* (1997), and *The Matrix* (1999) had drawn huge crowds but after that, they began to be dubbed, and effectively became Tamil movies that other theatres could also screen. Customers now had the option to watch the same movies in more modern, renovated theatres with better air-conditioning. Still, the staff were loyal. Mr Veera, who has been running the concession stand at Rathna for nearly twenty years, learned his first English words working there. His favourite flicks are the 'science' movies like *Independence Day* (1996) and *Armageddon* (1998).

Thribhuvan believes that Pondicherry's epicentre is here, at the movies. When the film buff is not greeting customers, checking ticket sales, or having a discussion with Vinod in the projection room, he likes to perch on the roof of the building and observe movement in and out of it. 'In my theatre,' he says, 'every day, the audience has to go inside four times, and they have to come out four times. You time lapse it, over four months, over a year, and you'll see it.' Thribhuvan closes his hand into a fist and pumps it. 'That's the heartbeat.'

Having lost its English-only edge, Rathna began

purchasing Tamil and Hindi films, many of which flopped in the theatres. Unable to earn enough in ticket revenue, the theatre was badly affected. As more movies went to DVD, and customers had the choice to watch them in the comfort of their own home, the number of theatres in the city shrank to just five. Thribhuvan pumps his fist again. 'I felt at that time, this has to come alive again.'

Rathna closed for nearly four years between 2008 and 2012. The family invested in upgrades of all kinds, and transitioned into digital projection. 'We still have the old machines,' Thribhuvan says wistfully.

'Once we became AC, new pumped-up energy came in.' Thribhuvan's voice rises and falls as he narrates stories of customers begging for tickets before superstar Rajnikaanth's 2016 blockbuster *Kabali*, and his daredevil solutions to give every small-time politician and gangster—including Bass—a ticket for the show of their choice. He is equally excited about the renovations his family has made to their theatre. Thribhuvan points to an overhead shelter at the entrance of the movie hall, and explains that it was constructed to prevent a glare from hitting the screen whenever someone opened a door into the hall.

Could this just as easily be Chennai, or any movie theatre in Tamil Nadu? Thribhuvan is protective. Rathna must have a different life from standard local theatre culture. When Pondy crowds are thick and frenzied, as before the first screening of *Kabali*, Thribhuvan is on alert: women and families enter first and find their seats. Then the masses are let in, loud and restless. This cultural bastion on the boulevard, this heartbeat, must represent the city's voices, stories and dreams in namma bhaashai, our language. For Thribhuvan, this translates to the dozens of scripts and movies he wants to create for Tamil cinema. Because if he doesn't create them when he has the perfect venue for them, then who will? 'I was sitting inside the theatre after the last show, I was all alone, I put on some music for myself, and it was then I realized what I've been given. How many directors in this world have a theatre just for themselves? I *do* see big things in Rathna. I see myself dying in Rathna. Like *Cinema Paradiso* (1998). Sitting at Rathna, looking back at my life, the movies I had made, and finally just having a painless heart attack and going in peace. A bit dramatic, but so what!'

÷

About fifteen minutes north of Rathna, beyond the boulevards and off the East Coast Road (ECR) highway stands another tall building. Its sign is also in plain capital letters, its name another catchy two-syllable word. Satya Special School was founded in 2003 and caters to children with a range of physical and mental disabilities. Headquartered here, it has centres in urban and rural parts of the union territory, including a Mobile Therapy Unit which conducts 'home based services to over 124 disabled children' in 44 rural villages. Satya works with nearly 800 children; addressing not only their needs, but also educating their families and even providing microcredit to enterprising mothers.

The original enterprising mother is Chitra Shah. She is endlessly energetic, even at 7.30 in the morning. I meet her at a vegetarian restaurant on Nehru Street. She first orders breakfast and coffee, confirms that I understand Tamil, and then plunges into the story of her life. Long hair frames her round face, and she wears a small pottu on her forehead. Shah's family had considered her a 'chamathu Chennai girl' (which is where she's from)—well-behaved and studious—who had opted for a master's degree in biochemistry 'because that was the in thing' in the eighties. But on the very first day of the course, she found herself uninterested, and wandered across the street to the Indian Institute of Technology (IIT) Madras, and into a career counselling session. Listening to a professor of Social Work speak passionately about the profession, Shah was inspired. 'I quietly went in and filled in my application, did a group discussion, and got into a master's in Social Work. I came home and my dad said: "What kind of a family have you come from? How can you work in the slum?" My aunt said, "To work in the slum, why do you have to get a master's? What a waste of my brother's resources!"'

Rejecting her elders' advice, Shah charged ahead. Exposed to the horrors of bride burning, prostitution and female infanticide, she became a 'hardcore feminist'.

47

During fieldwork in Tamil Nadu, she met countless women farmers who willingly killed their own girl children, poisoning or drowning them to save them from destitute futures. Shah saw success and failure in different schemes, from the Cradle Baby Scheme launched by the Tamil Nadu government in 1992—which is still in effect today—to foiled attempts to rescue and rehabilitate sex workers. These inspired her and discouraged her, but never exhausted her drive to help the women.

Marriage brought Shah to Pondicherry, where her husband is a prominent industrialist. His family is attached to Sri Aurobindo Ashram. When she first moved from the bustle of Chennai to sleepy Pondicherry, without a job to keep her busy, she did not know what to do with herself. Studying Sri Aurobindo's philosophy only made her more restless. 'I tried reading—nejjamaave, really—made a serious effort. Supramental manifestation was not my cup of tea!'

She began volunteering with a psychiatrist, and helping him round up children with special needs who required counselling. Dr Surendran had earlier been with the University of Glasgow in the UK, and was an alumni of JIPMER. 'That is one of the reasons why he came back [to India] to practice.' Shah interrupts her story to order: 'Rendu coffee, strong coffee-aa?' confirming with the waiter that the tumblers will contain more decoction than milk. 'This was his free clinic and every Wednesday was his clinic for children with special needs.

There was this girl with Down Syndrome, about thirteen years old, who caught our attention. She came with cut marks on her arms and legs and Dr Surendran called me and said, "You want some excitement in life? This is the address of the child, go do a house visit." He thought there was some kind of abuse, but he couldn't understand what was happening; she was a non-verbal kid. I said okay, took down the address, then told [her husband's] driver, we have to go here. He said, "I won't take you there!" I said why? He said, "Does Ayya know?" I told him this won't work. If you don't take me, I will take an auto! He said, "No auto will go there!" I said, "If you don't take me, I'll go on my own, somehow.'"

Shah found herself in a Narikurava community, an indigenous people with scant education and earning opportunities, who lived in a village 'near the Pondy dump yard'. The address Shah had been sent to, a windowless shack with mud walls, emitted even worse smells. Inside, the girl she had last met in the office was tied to a plastic chair with nylon ropes, sitting in her own filth, a plate of fly-covered food on a nearby table, and 'one koda-koda-koda fan', Shah describes, imitating the rattle of the blades. She adds a spoon of sugar to her coffee and pours it back and forth before taking a sip and continuing her story.

The girl's mother, it turned out, had nowhere to leave her daughter while she worked at a construction site. Leaving her with a relative had gotten the girl

49

pregnant *twice*, and bringing her to work had set the boss's eyes on her. Shah was speechless as the mother continued. 'And she says, "What do you think, I'm the only mother who does this?" And I said, "You know more mothers like this?" She says, "I know 20-30 more mothers like this!" I freaked out. This can't be true. Then I realized—this is reality.'

That encounter grew into a much larger project that Shah, tireless and relentless, envisioned as a programme, a community where children with special needs and their parents could come and seek the proper help they needed. From disabusing parents of notions that lightning could cure disability, and trying to rationalize with frustrated fathers that a child's disability was not a reason to drink away the family's income, to growing a small office into a multi-storey building and outfitting it with a one-of-a-kind wheelchair-accessible playground, Shah has spent over twenty years building Satya Special School into an incredible programme in Pondicherry. Mothers—and occasionally fathers—accompany their children to school to learn the various therapies required to take care of them. The children learn academic and vocational skills; sports and physio trainers conduct workshops with the children and parents; and unlike the mud-walled hut where Shah encountered a desperate mother and daughter, here, the overwhelming emotion is pride.

In 2013, Satya sent four athletes to participate in the Special Olympics Asia Pacific Games in Newcastle,

Australia, in basketball and athletics. 'It was quite a story,' Shah says, swilling the dregs of her coffee and calling for the bill. Shah's athletes were from a small village and, even in 2013, Pondicherry wasn't enough of a city to prepare them for Australia. At the time there were no escalators in Pondicherry, so 'we used to take them to Chennai to get them used to an escalator, we used to take them to a mall. They had never seen escalators!' Three of the children—a bus driver's son; a shop vendor's daughter; a farmer's daughter—had no funds to cover their expenses and there was no government support, 'though these kids went as part of the Indian contingent'. Satya coughed up the ₹60,000 per athlete that was required, and the children returned with gold medals in basketball and track and field.

Shah's medal-deserving efforts have made Pondicherry aware of, and sensitive to, those with special needs. A year earlier, in 2012, she managed to include some of Satya's mothers in the annual 'Ability Night' programme at Pondicherry University, which showcases the talents of people with special needs. The song 'Jai Ho' from the movie *Slumdog Millionaire* was popular at the time, and the mothers came and said, 'Aadanum pola irruku', we feel like dancing to this song. Shah smiles. 'These mothers went on stage and danced. And you should have seen them after their performance. Some of them came to me and said, "We literally feel like we had wings, and we could fly." That was solid empowerment.'

Their confidence soared for days after that. Earlier, they were ashamed to be seen in public; the older girls with special needs would complain, 'Ennaka pidikela, I don't like it, everyone is looking at me.' But now, their mothers felt ready to face the world. 'The next week, they came and asked, "Can we all go for a walk on the beach?' Shah agreed. "Let's all go as a gang." Ten of them, their children, a huge group, started walking. I had told my staff: if you think somebody is staring a little more than they should, walk up to them and say, do you want to know more about our condition? We'll talk to you about it. It did happen, we did walk up to a couple of them. Some of them were interested in knowing, some were, ille ille—no, no—and wanted to slip away. But at least people started seeing us.'

From ECR to the city's boulevards, look out for Shah and her 'gang' of mothers and children. They may not be jogging, they may not be taking selfies, they may not stop to watch a game of pétanque. But they march up and down the Promenade with as much right as anyone else there. Shah has made sure of that.

÷

Vani likes to dress up before an evening walk and dinner in White Town. In shiny, dark red lipstick, her hair in a half-ponytail, carrying a purse to match her outfit, she arrives at the restaurant on her two-wheeler. Dinner is standard South Indian fare—dosai and sambar—which she interrupts to call her boyfriend Dharun, who lives in America, and for whom it is now morning. She pouts slightly before speaking into the phone, her Tamil fluent, her English careful, and her voice trills with excitement as she hands her phone to me so I can say hello. Dinner ends with a squabble over who should pay the bill. I win, and Vani is only mollified when we agree she will cover the dessert afterwards. At Richy Rich a few blocks away, Vani's parents and baby nephew join; their foreheads are colourful after a temple visit, where they have been praying for Dharun: that he may successfully complete his studies in America, come back to Pondicherry, and marry their daughter. Everyone orders ice cream.

Vani's family lives just beyond the canal, on Rue Cazy in the Muslim Quarter. Up two flights of stairs is her family's ₹6,000-per-month rented apartment. A long hallway opens into a living room, and beyond that, the kitchen and a bathroom. The corridor is ideal for her nephew, whom Vani picks up daily from playschool and brings home. She and her mother took care of him before her older sister and brother-in-law fetch him after their work day. He runs happily between the main door and the living room, chasing a ball or playing hide-and-seek with his aunt. Every morning his grandmother, Vani's mother, quickly makes lunch and packs some for her husband, who handles the morning shift at their stall on Rue Victor Simonel, just opposite the General Hospital, and adjacent to Bharati Park. Selling packaged goods and bottled water, they cater to passers-by who

53

prefer the more hygienic, sealed packets of chips to the freshly-made pakodas in the next stall. I meet them at their stall in the evening. Both husband and wife have a knack for striking up conversation, so long as it is in namma bhaashai; they don't speak English or French. They are delighted to meet someone who has come from New York; their son-in-law-to-be is studying there, too, although they don't know the name of the university. Come back tomorrow, they insist, by which time they will have found out and can let me know.

Vani has inherited her mother's garrulousness and close-set eyes. In her early twenties, she is interminably in awe of a world beyond Pondicherry. She grew up here, and completed her bachelor's in engineering at Manakula Vinayagar College, an hour west of the beach in Madagadipet. She is bright and vivacious, but is resisting employment for now. 'I'm just staying at home. Waiting for my boyfriend, to get married, and then I'll go to America to look for a job.' Drying her hair vigorously with a towel, she re-ties it in a knot on her head so she can converse and gesture at the same time. Among her university cohort of fifty-nine, she continues, many have moved to Chennai, Bangalore, and parts of Kerala for jobs. Some have made it to the US and to Singapore with technology companies. 'Only *my* boyfriend went to do a master's,' she says, blushing. He is at SUNY Binghamton—she stumbles over the syllables—in New York—she emphasizes this—and it isn't worth clarifying to her that SUNY is over 300 kilometres away from New York City, where she dreams of living someday. She wants to be an anchor. 'I'm always talking! Are there Tamil channels in America? Music? Sun TV? Vijay TV?'

With parents who run a small shop, a married and working older sister, and an engineering degree of her own, Vani is typical in that she is ambitious but also naïve. She wants to get married, she wants to work, and until she does both, she happily helps out at home and takes care of her nephew. Pinning her hopes on a boyfriend abroad, she believes in the future they have built over many conversations in college and Skype calls. But where the story sounds less typical is when her parents chime in, fully supportive of their younger daughter's relationship and life decisions. Dharun's family is also based in Pondicherry, and he is a nalla payyain, a good boy. The relationship has been going on since Vani went to college three years earlier, and her parents have grown used to seeing him around the house in the past few years; moonu-naalu varsham ippo pazhakkam. We like him very much, Vani's mother says; we've already begun calling him namma veetu pillai, part of the family. They are clear that their daughter will have a 'love marriage'.

Perhaps because Pondicherry is that contradiction of being a small town with lots of cultural capital, Vani is like many other Tamil twenty-somethings, and also unlike them. Her friends, for example, include classmates from college, neighbours, and an American

55

named John who is in his sixties. 'He's staying here for a year. He's writing about something, maybe Arabindo Ashram.' She swipes to a picture of them on her phone. 'He doesn't speak Tamil, so he calls me to help him translate. He's from California. But I like New York— because my boyfriend is staying there!'

Does Vani know anything about the Aurobindo Ashram? Does she ever visit? She is firm in her response. 'The Ashram does its own thing. They do everything separately, stay separately. [People] come from all over other states, and do their own thing. Each one's background if you see, are big people, periya aal. But they leave everything. They give all their possessions to the Ashram. They stay in White Town, in the Ashram.'

Vani's guide to her city is a reflection of her age, comfort zones and preferences. In a rapid-fire question-and-answer session, she prepares a sightseeing itinerary for me: 'Have you seen the Old Lighthouse? Yes, you *can* go to the top.' When her mother reminds her that the Lighthouse is closed, she isn't deterred. 'Oh—you can't? Then I guess they changed that recently. But we can ask and go!' She ranks the city's schools without a second thought. 'Cluny [Convent] and Petit [Seminaire] are *bestest* schools. Then Patrick School—you know MH hospital, it's on the backside. Immaculate [Heart of Mary Girls School] is okay, but not as high-tech as the other four.' As for Tagore Arts College, which was prestigious back in the sixties and seventies, Vani is far less kind. 'Adhellaan poyachu! That's long gone! At the university level, enga college thaan number one—for computer science, my college is by far the best.'

What about Rathna Theatre? Does she watch movies there? Vani doesn't recognize the name, and asks her mother. 'They've taken it down,' her mother declares. 'Now there's an office there.' This, too, seems unworthy of correction.

Does Vani have cousins nearby? Chennai, she says, and they love to visit. Why? She grins. 'Sarakku!' Alcohol!

Her Pondicherry extends far beyond the boulevards and she offers her two-wheeler for longer distance journeys: 'Auroville? Aurobeach? The roads are good. Pondicherry is always neat and clean.' And if I want to relax, then she recommends 'Le Pondy', which she calls 'lay Pondy'. Self-described as a 'premium leisure resort beautifully lounged at an estuary between Chunnambar River and the Bay of Bengal', the resort advertises 'Pondicherry in all its true sense—the spirit, the architecture and the revelry'.

With restaurants, pools, and picturesque views of the water, it's easy to see why a romantically-inclined young woman is so captivated by Le Pondy. 'In Pondicherry, it's the best place!' she promises.

Most of Vani's outings—when Dharun isn't around—have been with family, and that usually means temples. Here, too, Vani has suggestions. 'Aanjaneyar Temple. Kali Kovil.' Both are outside of the city, which shows the family's piety, since Pondicherry itself is full

57

of temples. Aanjaneyar, or Hanuman, is revered for his bold, ocean-spanning adventures, and Kali is the fearless feminine divine. Both neatly sum up Vani's long-term hopes.

÷

Meeting these diverse people has shown me that Black Town and White Town are two halves of the same city. Tamil and French are both mother tongues. Religious life thrives on either side of the canal, including that most sacred and secular daily ritual of the walk on the Promenade. And each boasts a neighbourhood 'poet and nationalist': Subramania Bharati from the south, and Aurobindo Ghose from the north both arrived in Pondicherry in the first decade of the twentieth century. They were both fleeing the British, and both left literary legacies within the boulevards.

Bharati lived in Pondicherry from 1908 to 1918. Like Sri Aurobindo, he moved around a few times before settling down—to stay hidden from the authorities—and his final residence was on Eswaran Kovil Street, in the Tamil section of town. He was arrested in 1918, and spent nearly a month in a Cuddalore Jail, just across the border in Tamil Nadu, before quitting Pondicherry for good. His house, which fell into disrepair after that, was renovated in 2016 and converted into a museum-cum-research centre where anyone can read Bharati's letters, articles and poetry.

Even though he lived only until thirty-nine, Bharati

had been writing poems since he was seven; his oeuvre covered 'patriotic verses, poems on national integration and education, poems against casteism, untouchability, social evils and oppression, poems written for children, and devotional songs'. Born in 1882 and raised in Tamil Nadu, he would skip school as a young boy to 'roam in the fields, absorbed in nature, listen to the folk songs of the peasants, or study the works of Tamil poets'. That wonderment stayed with him when he studied Sanskrit and Hindi in Banaras Hindu University, and he returned to the south to continue writing poetry. He also forayed into newspaper and magazine writing, and served as editor for different Tamil publications in Chennai. He quit those in 1906 to join *India*, a brand-new Tamil weekly, as its editor. And when the British stopped the magazine in 1908 and arrested one of its editors, Bharati quit Chennai for Pondicherry (since it was exempt from British jurisdiction), hoping to continue publishing *India*. The vernacular magazine's motto was 'Liberty, Equality, Fraternity', inspired by the French Revolution—another example of Pondicherry's Tamil-French double helix.

By now Bharati had met fellow activists Bal Gangadhar Tilak, Lala Lajpat Rai, and Aurobindo Ghose at Congress meetings in the north, and published their words in *India*. He arrived in Pondicherry at the same time that Ghose was arrested in Calcutta. Besides *India*, Bharati was the editor of *Vijaya*, a daily newspaper, as well *Karma Yogi*, a Tamil monthly. The

59

latter published Ghose just before he went into hiding in Bengal and turned up in Pondicherry a month later, having travelled south in secret, by ship.

Not surprisingly, Bharati and Ghose became good friends in their shared exile in Pondicherry. They were also incredibly prolific, each on a journey to unite their people and sing for their nation. As if in dialogue with Ghose's northern origins, Bharati writes, in 'Bharat Desh':

> We shall swap the wheat of the Gangetic plains
> for the tender betel leaves of the Kaveri basin
> We shall honour the poets of the valiant
> Marathas
> with gifts of ivory from Kerala
> [...]
> sitting at Kanchi we will listen to
> the discourses of scholars in Varanasi
> [...]
>
> With the name of Bharat Desh on our lips
> let us shake off our fears and poverty.

While in Pondicherry, both men composed epic poems about fearless women in Hindu mythology. Bharati wrote *Panchali Sabatham*, about Panchali, or Draupadi, wife of the Pandavas. Sri Aurobindo wrote *Savitri*—so famous in the Ashram that Heehs refers to it as 'that epic in iambic pentameter'—about a Hindu princess, Savitri, who confronted Yama, God of Death, to win her husband back from the underworld. A 2009 edition of the poem, published by the Sri Aurobindo Ashram Publications Department, is over 700 pages long.

Just as mythology inspires poetry, so does faith. Bharati wrote the poem 'Allah', describing him as 'the power behind / the ceaseless movement of millions upon / millions of galaxies in infinite space'. In 'Yesu Kiristu', Bharati praises Christ's sacrifice on the cross:

> My countrymen! Listen to the inner meaning of this event:
> God will enter our hearts and protect us from all evils, every day, if we destroy our egotism, our arrogance.

Bharati grounded his poetry and idealism in concrete, tangible visuals. No matter how lofty his thoughts, he phrased them in simple, direct Tamil. And having written so much while in Pondicherry, it is inevitable, says Aneesh Raghavan, that the city's earth, music and spirit seeped into his words. Raghavan is a doctoral student in Sanskrit, an Odissi dancer and an amateur Carnatic musician who has studied Bharati's work for its many connections to his academic and artistic pursuits. He delights in every mention of Pondicherry in Bharati's writings. For example, in a love poem to his wife, 'Maalai Pozhudhiloru Maedai', the poet is sitting on an elevation overlooking the sea and gazing into the distance. Raghavan interprets the setting as Pondicherry's old pier: 'Whenever [Bharati] imagined an ideal town, or had to express the concept of a community of people, he used the word "Vedapuri", which was the name of Pondicherry.' Raghavan quotes the poem 'Pudiya Konangi', or 'New Fortune Teller', that begins 'Gudugudu gudugudu gudugudu gudugudu / Happy days ahead for the people!'

'You've heard of this gudugudu kaaran?' Raghavan asks, referring to the local fortune tellers who used to rattle their hand-held drums and make a 'gudugudu' sound, while walking around the neighbourhood and making pronouncements about the future. Bharati's 'gudugudu kaaran' predicts great things for Pondicherry:

> Caste feelings are no more.
> No more are there any conflicts.
> Shakti! Maha Kali! Speak up!
> Predict good times for the people of Vedapura!

Bharati is saying, 'Wake up oh Vedapuri, this is going to happen to you: people are going to be more receptive to higher qualities,' Raghavan translates. This sentiment, along with Bharati's fiery, colloquial eloquence, has been adopted by Tamil Nadu politicians, turned into film songs, and used to celebrate the Tamil language; his poetry is regularly quoted by locals and leaders alike.

There are several bookshelves in Bharati's Eswaran Kovil Street home in the Tamil Quarter that hold a thoroughly catalogued bibliography of the Renaissance man. Renovated using government funds and INTACH expertise, it is now a proud tribute to the house's

Tamil and French architecture—another instance of the double-helix—with a mix of exhibits and archives.

Pondicherry's DNA, if one can stretch the metaphor, is necessarily multi-dimensional. Neither black nor white, it is both. Neither French nor Tamil, it is both. Neither spiritual nor secular, it is both. Attribute this to the siddha's subterranean divine energy, or to the Alliance Française's propagation of French to locals and visitors, or to businessman Dilip Kapur's theory that French Pondicherry, Tamil culture and the Ashram can coexist because of how tolerant the Tamil community is. But I prefer not to choose one theory over another, for the same reason that genes are most compelling in their aggregate: that is when they create a complete personality.

63

Thribhuvan, Shah, Vani and Bharati aren't all that different in their aspirations to connect with others, exercise their independence, and promote cheerfulness around them. One uses movies, another medical awareness, a third romance, and Bharati, of course, poetry. This sentiment could have come from any of them: 'I want to sow an idea that will reap millennia of wisdom in people's minds.' But then the second line reveals the speaker's identity, and although only he could have said this, his meaning is just as tightly coiled around that double helix as everyone else's:

'I just want them to walk out of my theatre, silent.'

FIVE

Called to Prayer

Sound before light. The muezzin's voice seeps in through windows and spills into the ears of the wakeful and the sleeping. It is still dark outside as the Muslim call to prayer spreads over Pondicherry's sky. Some morning walkers use this as their alarm clock to gather on the Promenade, which is also quiet, carrying only the sound of human feet and ocean waves. The sun begins to rise, first a muted smear behind clouds, orange and pink and blue. Then suddenly it becomes a too-bright golden spear of light.

Just a few blocks from the Promenade, still in White Town, Celclia is on her terrace for her morning exercise. She completes several rounds of surya namaskar to get the blessings of 'Surya, and then Mother Mary'. She points east at the water, for the sun god, and then turns around to point at the statue of the Virgin Mary that sits on the top of the Church of Immaculate Conception a few more streets inland. She finishes her yoga with her hands folded in prayer, first facing the sun, next, the Virgin Mary. Then it's time for laps of her terrace, in figure eights, to keep her knees flexible. 'I have to walk up and down these stairs all the time,' she says, in Tamil, about the building she lives in. 'It's important to give my legs exercise.'

Back on the Promenade, walkers are filling the street. Their conversations rise like prayers into the morning air. The Eglise de Notre Dame des Anges, iconic for its pink walls and tall towers, responds with morning church bells. Less conspicuous from the beach, temples and mosques scattered throughout the city begin their morning activities. At 7.30 a.m., the boulevard erupts with growling engines and shrill horns too syncopated to be a soothing chant or an invigorating prayer. But with their arrival, a new meditation begins, focused on academic and professional success.

For the next hour, 'first period' is starting in several convent schools and students are reciting prayers in chorus. In Knowledge, Sri Aurobindo Ashram students begin their college-level courses only after the classroom speakers have broadcast a morning melody composed by the Mother, Sri Aurobindo's former disciple, who was later elevated to his spiritual partner and Ashram leader. The music is atmospheric, chords merging into one another, sounding rather like the soundtrack of a science-fiction movie. It lasts at least two minutes, during which all the students bow their heads in silence.

At 10 a.m., there is considerable bustle in the Manakula Vinayagar Kovil in White Town. One of the oldest sites of worship in Pondicherry—about 300 years old and, uniquely, predating the French—it is dedicated to Ganesha, the popular elephant-headed son of Parvathi and Shiva. Nowadays, there is hardly a moment when the temple isn't full of visitors. But in the early seventies, those living near the temple barely heard its rituals. There were a few daily visitors, but that was it; the priests even knew devotees by name back then.

The day heats up, blazing onto the streets and diffusing the already thinning sea breeze. All that early-morning fervour has faded—thoughts veer towards lunch, shade, repose. On a Saturday, the Ashram school operates a half-day of classes. After her Spanish language class, teacher Lata Jauhar bolts the school gate shut. As she stands at the large door, rotating a long key in the lock, the smell of mallipoo—jasmine flowers—hangs heavy and tempting in the air, disorienting me. Across the street, women on street corners are making and selling mallipoo garlands, calling out to pedestrians in the hope that they are headed to the Manakula Vinayagar Kovil and need flowers. It is yet another Pondy moment for me: that Spanish music, the end of the school week, and a visit to the temple can fuse into a single fragrant moment.

Post-lunch, while many are preparing to return to their place of work, a few religious men and women meet in the cool silence of another kovil. This time it is a Christian Maatha Kovil, about fifteen minutes away from the Ganesha temple, and similarly senior in status. The Immaculate Conception Cathedral was first built by the French in 1692, and had to be rebuilt four more times after it was razed to the ground once by the Dutch and then by the British some time later. It was most recently completed in 1791. The year 2017 marked the 325th anniversary of the first church erected on this site, and the 225th anniversary of the current construction.

Resplendent in a white and gold facade, the cathedral is a dignified sight. A statue of the Virgin Mary graces the courtyard in front of the monument, and welcomes anyone off the road. Mission Street is subtitled on road signs as 'Rue des Mission Etrangères' and 'Rue de la Cathédrale', signalling, respectively, the Jesuits and Capuchins, and the cathedrals that have been associated with this street for three centuries. Today, Immaculate Conception is the 'mother church for the Roman Catholic Archdiocese of Pondicherry'; it houses the Archbishop Rev. Dr Antony Anandarayar.

'His governing territory goes up to Coimbatore,' Raj clarifies, who is part of a ... group that convenes in the church every afternoon from 2.30 to 4 p.m. Sometimes three and sometimes more, they sit still and silent, quiescent in the semi-...ness, small underne... enormous stained-glass wi...ws, ...ressed pillars, the altar itself. Celclia ... ...e of t... group, an... invited me to participa... ...up is well-verse... ...ers Not surprisingly, ... Roman Catholic ...the history of the chur...iastical province of India—known ...

...lic
...that it
...religions
...quirement to
the Ashram. And
...nt of ashramites and
...tsider.

...lly against it. They have a
...mites have to get married to

Raj: No, no. They can't marry.
...hine: They can, but they cannot marry an
the Ashram.
Raj: No, no, they can't marry at all.
Josephine: If they get married, they are out of the Ashram.
Raj: If you get married, you are out of the Ashram. Automatically.

Josephine: I am totally against it!
Raj: The thing is, they don't g...
...property. I know one of my very ...
that is, after he became an ashramit... very well. He was very filthy rich. ...
married a JIPMER doctor.
Josephine: Out of the Ashram.
Raj: She was sent out of the Ashram. T...
way they function.
Josephine: But it's a beautiful place. Pe...

68

various congregations in Pondicherry. Raj answers questions keenly, in fluent English, which is why Celclia has introduced him to me. His wife Josephine sometimes interrupts him to explain aspects of their religion, alternately competing with, and confirming, her husband's devoutness. He is tall and burly, while she is petite and sports short hair; their opposites perfectly complement a partnership solidified in faith.

Raj, Josephine and Celclia are proud of the churches and congregations in Pondicherry, and the influence they have had on the city. Apart from particular multiculturalism, there is a certain unity in the treatment of others.

Pondicherry's open-mindedness is visible during annual festivals. 'If you see during Christmas, lots of Hindus and ashramites come to our church,' Raj says. 'People of other religion they come here, and we welcome them, enter them. It is not about converting or anything. They have great faith in Mother Mary. Unlike other areas, here is no religious intolerance here.'

Inter-religious marriage, however, brings up different opinions. Josephine confides that their daughter is in love with a Hindu and that Raj is against it. She, too, holds conditions 'I've made it very clear that he...wedded. [My dear] said "I'll...that. '[A Hindu...]...

70

What they do recommend is the Eglise des Anges as 'one more peaceful, beautiful...the beach. You must go in the evening,'...the first Friday of the month. Masses are co...daily in three languages: Tamil, English and French...only church in Pondicherry to cater to its polyphoni...vernacular. Built most recently in the 1850s, it, too, like the Immaculate Conception Cathedral, has been through several reconstructions. The local worshippers are, not surprisingly, very proud of both of these facts.

But there is still competition for visitors to experience a resounding evening mass, whether or not the sermon is in a language they follow. L'Eglise de Sacre Coeur de Jesus, or the Basilica of the Sacred Heart of Jesus, is a colourfully lit structure on Pondicherry's southern boulevard, facing the railway station. Completed only in 1908, and renovated in the 1960s, it is usually the brightest building on the street, visible from half a kilometre away with its string light decorations and music booming from inside.

Raj...
But wh...
is different...
senseless.

Josephine: We cann...
but I am against it, b...
Ashram; I'm not intereste...

The razzmatazz doesn't stop there. A booth towards the front of the church houses two sound engineers who monitor and broadcast the sermons and choir, ensuring total acoustic balance in all three wings of the church, as well as for the spillover audience seated in the courtyards outside. A television crew moves about near the altar to capture various angles of the many speakers—men and women, young and old—and knows when to pan to the audience who are equal parts entranced and daydreaming. The TV screens allow people in every corner to see the speakers' faces, and browse the announcements and commentary running across the bottom. For those who haven't made it to church that day, there is always the twenty-four-hour channel available online: Lourdes TV.

It is the first Friday of the month and everyone is in their best outfits. Seated in the pews, or on the floor around the pews (leaving hardly any walking room), the congregation glitters and shimmers in their saris, shirts, dupattas and frocks. The most conspicuous colour is red. Most of the women are in red crepe saris with ornate borders and patterns. With large red pottus on their foreheads, and fresh bunches of mallipoo in their hair, they look like any other Tamil Hindus. Their deities, too, are garlanded, like in the Hindu temples nearby; the Virgin Mary in a perfectly pleated sari looks unusual to me. But the sermon feels more standard, focusing on anbu, makkal and ozhukkam—love, people and virtue—and praising kadaval, aandavan, and Yesu:

71

god, lord, and Christ.

On signals from the priests delivering the sermon, the worshippers sit, stand and kneel. Some are barefoot; others keep their sandals on. The wings of the church seem to be filled mostly with women, only some men are visible. The rules of this mass are not immediately obvious, but the church's persona exudes excess more than constraint. Digital broadcasts and live television aside, the choir is reason enough to attend today's mass. The hymns are catchy, rhythmic, and Casio keyboard-enhanced; with each new song, the gumptious musical director introduces a new synthesizer setting, from the drums to the maracas.

The stained-glass panels are similarly flamboyant, and there's a reason for that, says Bishwajit Banik, who self-advertises as an alternative tour guide. 'I prefer oral history,' he says, to explain his research methods. Having grown up in Pondicherry and spoken to hundreds of locals, he learned that the inaugural priests in the church returned the original stained-glass sheets to the manufacturers in Italy, insisting on brighter colours and more vibrant depictions of Christ. The end result is somewhat psychedelic—not unlike all the colourful bulbs strung up on the church's exterior—and the apostles shown in these panels are buff, macho figurines. To explain this nearly gaudy show of devotion, Banik leads me around the church, past the Lourdes TV office, and through a small gate. This brings us to Rue Caron, part of a neighbourhood of streets formerly known as the Dalit area. Still set off from the rest of the city's café-with-free-WiFi-riddled streets, it is mostly residential—save one butcher's shop, his caged hens and roosters squawking loudly at passers-by—and redolent of a community that was left behind while the rest of the city underwent a transformation. In fact, as told by Banik, the story is the opposite.

÷

Over the eight years it took France to officially and completely transfer Pondicherry to India, the French government issued some 20,000 passports to its coastal citizens. Most of these were snapped up by poor, low-caste residents who had converted to Catholicism under their colonial rulers, and become very pious Christians, happy for all the benefits they now received under the French. In 1954, the French Army 'needed bodies' to strengthen their army with, and these same converts with fresh passports eagerly signed up, hopeful for a better, caste-free life abroad. Many joined the army as soldiers (soldats in French); others were given low-level government jobs, such as sweeping the streets or cleaning the airport. Those who made it to retirement age were then sent back to Pondicherry with a fat French pension, which was worth significantly more in India. By now it was the late 1960s and 1970s—a period of financial slump in India, under Indira Gandhi's license-permit-quota-raj policies—and these dark-skinned, French-speaking, foreign-returned, blue-collar families began resurrecting Pondicherry's economy.

Flush with money and pride, they marked their homes with updated nameplates, having chosen French names that did not indicate caste, like M et Mme Dragon. They painted their homes in bright colours for their bold, unapologetic tastes. And they remembered the church that had abutted their childhood homes, and decided to embellish it the same way. I read online that 'The Grotto for Our Lady of Lourdes, Parish Hall, Adoration chapel and the new parish community hall were some of the developments of this church since the 1960s', referring to a life-size replica of the Sanctuary of Our Lady of Lourdes that has been erected in the Basilica's courtyard. Indians who can't pilgrimage across the oceans to the south of France to witness this sight can, instead, take the train to Pondicherry.

Rue Caron turns into Rue Chermont, which forms a crossroads with Rue Latouche. Banik stands in the centre of the cross, arms and smile spread wide. 'This is Pondicherry. You have a church on one side, a mosque beyond it, and a temple on the other side. In the evenings you can hear all of them. It's a true Tower of Babel!'

÷

The Couthbapalli Mosque in the Muslim Quarter operates in two languages. 'Obviously,' the prayers are in Arabic, explains Indrani Singh Cassime, 'but the announcements are in Tamil.' Born and raised in Delhi in a Hindu family, Indrani married A. Sayed Mohamed

Cassime, a prominent Muslim in Pondicherry. She has since fully integrated into his extended family, speaks Tamil and cooks South Indian food. Although she has lived in Pondicherry for over fifteen years, she still describes herself as an outsider.

Having grown up in a completely different environment from a South Indian, Tamil, Muslim home, Indrani identifies her husband's family, and the larger community, as a distinct hybrid of Tamil and Muslim cultures. It starts in the deep roots her husband's family has in the city: his grandfather H. M. Cassime was Mayor of Pondicherry from 1956 to 1961, the critical time period when the French were leaving India. The Canal Road bears his name, although incorrectly spelt as H. M. Kassim. His son C. M. Achraff (pronounced Ashraf) was elected to the legislative assembly of Pondicherry in 1969 representing the Bussy Constituency; Bussy Street is one border of the Muslim Quarter. With father and son in politics, catering to their constituencies meant fluency in Tamil language, culture, customs and food.

75

This has been Indrani's experience too, even though her husband Sayed, Achraff's son, did not continue in politics. Instead, he manages one of the many family properties in the city, and is a well-known businessman. 'They are quite Tamilian in their thought process,' Indrani says about her husband and his relatives. 'Their day-to-day life is like what any general Tamil family will have: sambar, rice and rasam for meals, no chappals in the house. They speak only in Tamil, watch Tamil TV serials. My husband's family is very much only Tamil-speaking; they don't know Urdu at all. They learn Arabic to read the Quran.'

It makes sense, then, for these Pondicherry Muslims, that announcements at the mosque are in Tamil. Do they all live in the Muslim Quarter?

'This is where the Muslims live, lane-wise and family-wise,' Indrani responds, using a phrase I appreciate for how Pondicherrian it is. So much of the city's life is organized *lane-wise*: on a specific side of the canal; on a street named after a particular temple; inside or outside a boulevard.

'There is another area, Kottakuppam, on ECR,' she adds, referring to a town 5 kilometres north of Pondicherry, just across the border into Tamil Nadu, and also on the coast. 'There are a huge number of Muslim residents over there. A couple of mosques also.'

Indrani lives and socializes lane-wise. Festivals are celebrated lane-wise; cuisine varies lane-wise—not to mention being distinct from Tamil food cooked in Tamil Nadu. Indrani lists South Indian dishes I don't recognize because of their Malaysian influences; luckily they are spelt out in *The Pondicherry Kitchen*, a popular cookbook by Pondicherrian Lourdes Tirouvanziam-Louis whose 'father was a Tamil-speaking, French-educated medical practitioner', and whose 'mother was a Vietnamese'. Referring to the Sisters of St. Joseph of Cluny Convent that sent missionaries to India in

1827 to 'take up education in Pondicherry', Indrani says that some Cluny sisters live 'five lanes away [and] keep visiting, and they eat the food that we prepare in these lanes'.

In that respect, the Muslim Quarter is porous. During Ramzan, 'everybody has iftar', Indrani says. 'We throw an iftar party and we call everyone, not just Muslims. I call my friend and her son, because we make vadai and chutney, which they like. They are Hindus. It's quite open and interactive. At Christmas, we receive gifts; Diwali, we receive sweets. On Eid, we make and send food to everyone. Everybody does this. For marriages, also, everybody invites everyone.'

What about inter-marriage?

'That never happens,' she says, simultaneously confident and casual, even though she was raised Hindu. Perhaps this is the mark of a multi-lingual, multi-religious, Sri Aurobindo Ashram-affiliated woman— who is also an artist and potter. In other words, this is how Pondicherrians speak about themselves. The Muslims here are culturally tolerant, religiously punctilious, linguistically Tamil, maritally strict and live lane-wise—and that's just the way it is, nothing good or bad, right or wrong about it.

÷

Reverend Father A. S. Antonisamy is another advocate for Pondicherry's religious porousness. In 1987, he 'initiated', in his words, the Inter-Religious Fraternal

Community, which still operates in the city today. Having arrived in the city in 1969, after completing his seminary training in Cuddalore, he served as a priest for nearly twenty years. As Pondicherry grew in the seventies and eighties, he felt that there could be greater fraternity between the different religious communities, which, today, is 87 per cent Hindu, and about 6 per cent Christian and 6 per cent Muslim.

Although he had toyed with the idea for some time, the spark came when one of the government secondary schools in Pondicherry was re-named after Father Beschi (pronounced Bes-kee), an Italian priest. The foreign missionary had arrived in Madurai, Tamil Nadu, in 1711 with a group of fellow Jesuits, and besides doing service had also learnt Tamil. He was so prolific in this new language that he was given the Tamil name Veeramamunivar, a bold, great and worldly-wise man. But Beschi Higher Secondary School, in Villupuram district outside the boulevards, did not have connections to any of the missions and convents that were instituted in Pondicherry. So why the school's christening? Antonisamy's interest was piqued.

He asked around, and found out that the idea had come from 'a Hindu, Siva Kannappa—a Tamil writer'. Antonisamy was surprised, so he went to the school to visit Kannappa and 'appreciate him'. Kannappa's rationale was that Father Beschi had made meaningful contributions to Tamil literature, and renaming a school was one way to honour his prose and poetry.

78

Antonisamy agreed: 'people should have that broad mind'.

He wondered whether there were members of the Muslim community who practiced this kind of inclusiveness. Kannappa said he had such a friend. Antonisamy asked if they could meet him, and Kannappa agreed boldly and confidently. 'In Tamil there is a very good expression [for this attitude]: dhaaraalamaa!'

Kannappa's friend was not only religious, but he was also the local caziar, or Muslim leader, named Mohamad Hussain. 'He was an educated man. He was even a member of the [legislative] assembly. Such a man, knowing that a priest is coming to his house, was so enthusiastic. We both of us went by cycle—those days only cycle!—in those Muslim streets. It was the first time we were going through those streets; people were curiously watching us. We met his friends and relatives, and found that he was a very good person.'

Antonisamy shared his idea for an inter-religious brotherhood, so far inchoate, with his two new friends. 'We are three [of us]; now we are happy. Why not we find people like us, who are open-minded. Two [friends] each. They said, "Yes, very good!" You know that Tamil expression, "Nalla yosanai, dhaaraalamaa seiyyalaam!" It's a good idea, we can definitely do it.'

Several meetings followed, in Antonisamy's office, the caziar's house, and retired Justice Ramalingam's house, a prominent Hindu whom Kannappa had also introduced Antonisamy to. The Father recalls the portrait of Bharati hung up in 'the house of the Hindu'. Criss-crossing town to make these visits, the three were struck by the city's segregated layout. 'Of course, there's the British system of "divide and rule"; the French system was more peaceful.' Antonisamy laughs and his eyebrows raise slightly, as if he is surprised by his own humour.

Soon the nine initial members—three from each religion—had assembled and decided they would build an 'inter-religious friendship movement'. The movement's motto is self-explanatory, he says. 'The process is friendship.' There would be a president, a vice president and a secretary, each from a different religion. All members would financially contribute, and use the funds to plan inclusive activities during the religions' major festivals. 'We should celebrate meals together: Christmas; Diwali; Eid.' Anyone could join, but to become members, they had to be 'three in one': three people of different faiths. In 1987, the president was Muslim, the vice president was Hindu and Antonisamy was the first secretary.

Their mission features five values. The first one, common to all three groups, is belief and faith in God. The remaining four come from the Indian Constitution: justice, equality, freedom, and fraternity. 'These five values we promote. That was our aim and objective. And we serve the poor. Whatever anybody is doing, we try to support them.'

The first few years were busy. Near Ousteri Lake,

the organization set up a rehabilitation home for the mentally ill called the Fraternal Life Community. They created a school for dropouts and for youth who had never made it into a classroom before, and raised money to fund all expenses. A few years passed, and then it was December 1992.

'You remember Babri Masjid was destroyed. We were able to settle things amicably.' Leaning forward in his chair, Antonisamy tells the story of the night of 6 December when, 'fortunately or unfortunately, I was sitting in a Muslim's house'. The television was on, and tuned to the BBC. They witnessed the mosque being attacked and destroyed, and instinctively Antonisamy knew that a singularly awful thing had befallen the country. 'Mosam pochu,' he says: something terrible had happened. He and the Imam immediately had the same thought, that at the mosque a few streets away, surely, tensions were mounting. Indeed, a large crowd had gathered, surrounded by police. 'But because of 144,' he explains, citing Section 144 of India's Criminal Procedure Code 'prohibit[ing] an assembly of more than five people in an area', nobody was taking action yet. It seemed only a matter of time before someone did, though. 'People were carrying instruments to do harm and destruction, especially youth. People were yelling.'

Justice Ramalingam had also arrived at the mosque. Antonisamy urged him to address the crowds as a fellow man of faith. 'I told the Hindu leader, you just tell what happened, how you came here. What you told me:

81

"nadakkadhadhu nadanda pochu", that which doesn't happen has happened. It's not all the Hindus who are responsible. You just tell that idea, and that we are with you.

'He used the mic which they use for the prayer call. Very simple man. And he said, "It's not all Hindus. There are few people who did it. But we'll do something together: what Father [Antonisamy] tells." Then I took the mic, just said "as-salaam-alaikum", but I don't know how to give peace to you.' The crowds listened, still saddened and helpless, but now sensing fraternity in their anguish and despair.

Antonisamy slept poorly that night. 'Then this thought came to me: God makes straight what is crooked. Man makes crooked what is straight. *Some* people have made India crooked; not all. God doesn't want to make it still more crooked. So we should do something to rectify. Something is broken, you have to paste it; if you break it more, what is the use.'

The leaders composed and signed a petition condemning the attack on the Babri Masjid. All nine of them went to speak to the Collector about the petition. The group requested that the local authorities pass a resolution to unanimously condemn the attack. They submitted their petition to Lieutenant Governor Har Swarup Singh. Pondicherrians felt placated by this. The police was relieved; politicians were attentive; the Fraternity Leadership was vocal. No violence erupted, within or without the boulevards.

'So that's how interreligious activity worked. Even if there is any problem now, they will ask us; the police, they will consult us. Any prayer meeting, we are invited. The government leader's birthday, they invite us. Gandhi Jayanti, we go together and we conduct a prayer.'

Behind Antonisamy's desk are a few picture frames. 'Our friendship: you can see the photos there. We are friends. The first two friends passed away, but again we renew our friendship. Now we have a fourth friend: a Jain. Faith is individual, that's okay. But friendship, you can have it with anybody. That's why, where there is love and friendship, there is God.'

÷

The evening is still young, and now some of the Hindu temples a short distance outside the city—many from the Chola dynasty, over 600 years old—are babbling with crowds who have come to attend dance festivals, witness the Masimagam processions to the Kuruchikuppam beach, or enjoy a harikatha concert where Hindu mythologies are shared in captivating, oral storytellings. But the most arresting temple for me is the Ayyanar Kovil in Mudaliarpet, about 5 kilometres southwest of the Promenade. Past the boulevards and the Botanical Gardens, it is tucked into a side street—helpfully named Ayyanar Kovil Street—and hidden from immediate view. Encounter the temple on a moonlit night and the towering statues, multi-limbed and formidable, come alive.

Ayyanar is a guardian deity. At various temples, he is shown seated with his wives, or on his horse, or at the end of a row of dogs, stick in hand and a robust moustache covering his face. Ayyanar temples are found at the entrance to Tamil villages, where the locals make offerings before setting off on a journey, and once again after they have returned safely. His shrines are also found in wilder settings, and have been studied by anthropologists and religion scholars as 'sacred groves' and 'forest shrines' that are prized for their 'significant [if not unlimited] conservation value'.

This Ayyanar Temple houses the standard Hindu deities, but presents them far more fantastically. Vishnu is seen in all his ten avatars; the massive statue contains the heads, bodies and tails of various animals, and human limbs that hold an assortment of weapons. The shrine to the nine planets has an intimidating chariot on its vimaanam—the sanctum's decorative roof—that is being driven by Surya the sun god, and pulled by several horses. If protection is this temple's identifier, it is apparent in the scale of the deities being prayed to.

Back in White Town, the Manakula Vinayagar Temple, conspicuous in Ashram territory, understands size, too. Its main attraction is the elephant, Lakshmi, who greets visitors at the temple entrance. Daily, Lakshmi is adorned with various decorations on her forehead, trunk and ears, which blithely flap about as she stands with her mahout and follows his instructions. Brave children and adults approach Lakshmi with money or grass, which Lakshmi curls her trunk around, and hands over to the mahout. She then bumps her trunk on the person's head by way of blessing. Offer too little money and Lakshmi won't accept it; too little grass and her trunk comes right back, poking around for more. She is a delight to behold in front of the temple, seemingly unaffected by the throngs passing by. While some remember the tradition of clambering on top of her, or standing next to her while a relative clicked a picture, others have started their own custom: selfies with Lakshmi.

Once the moon has settled in for the night, the kovil priests begin putting the pantheon to sleep. Eswaran Kovil Street, Perumal Kovil Street, Papammal Kovil Street, Muthumariamman Kovil Street, Kamatchi Amman Kovil Street—all parallel to each other, all on the other side of the canal, in the Hindu Quarter— quieten down. Instead, footsteps quicken towards the beach, into the French Quarter, where members of Sri Aurobindo Ashram can attend an exclusive late-night samadhi meditation session at 9 p.m., 'a place and construction for keeping in peace the bodies of Sri Aurobindo and the Mother'. Members scatter around the ever-silent garden and courtyard surrounding the two marble shrines: one for Sri Aurobindo, one for the Mother. Both are heaped with flowers that emit a hypnotic scent. All lights are off except for one lamp over the shrines, the tiny orange dots of the oodhavatti incense sticks burn down quickly, their smoky tails vanishing into the air along with people's prayers and thoughts.

If it is Ramzan, Muslims have long broken their fasts by now. Indrani has prepared varieties of dosais and chutneys that I have never eaten before. The churches stand dark and grand. Lakshmi the elephant has been led back to her stable. Shiva and Vishnu are asleep. But Ayyanar continues to keep watch, for the city is still awake. Restaurants and bars make their own, more hedonistic, offerings. Some strolling on the Promenade listen to the waves and ignore a father and son selling popcorn and hot chai. Theatres eject their late night viewers, whose scooters and motorbikes roar with the excitement of the movie. For there is sound before light. And tonight's fun before tomorrow's calls to prayer.

SIX

L'Option

Thanks to Lakshmi, 'my cousin is famous', says Rajendran. He pulls out his phone to swipe to a photo and check the date. '*The Hindu* wrote an article about him on 7 January 2016', reviewing his novel, *Carnet secret de Lakshmi*, about the temple elephant. Author Ari Gautier looks indistinguishable from the temple priests in the photo, all brown-skinned, black-haired, moustachioed men with sacred ash and vermillion on their foreheads. Indeed, he grew up in Pondicherry and studied at the Lycée Français, as so many locals do. Skimming the article, I'm puzzled by the connection between a published author named Gautier who lives in Norway, and Rajendran, who is sitting next to Bass and drinking a beer on the rooftop of Hotel Qualité, where the salty sea breeze mingles with the scent of marijuana from a nearby table.

'Meanwhile, I'm nearly forty and I'm not married,' he adds, responding to my unasked question. 'My father should have also taken French citizenship, and moved us all to France. Instead, I'm stuck here in India.'

This is the bizarre, but surprisingly common

dilemma of hundreds of families in Pondicherry who were separated by nationalities they inherited, adopted and renounced. Their stories begin nearly 200 years ago.

÷

In 1816, the French reclaimed Pondicherry from the British for the last time. They decreed, in an 1819 law, that the Indians in their territory were to be treated according to local Hindu governance, such as the laws of Manu, which maintained differences between upper and lower castes. They also recognized Hindus, Muslims and Christians differently. The French called these external policies 'mamool' (reinterpreting a Tamil word), which they applied to anyone who was not a French citizen.

But, by 1848, change was afoot in both empire and colony. With the establishment of the Second Republic in the former, attitudes toward the latter also shifted. France issued a decree that 'allowed the colonies representation in the national legislature', meaning that Indians who could prove at least five years of residency in a French territory were '[c]onsidered French whatever their religion or caste...[and] could have the same right as whites and persons of mixed race'. The locals, however, didn't translate 'liberté, égalité, fraternité' quite the same way. Upper castes refused to treat other communities equally, and there were terrible riots. The French government intervened by rescinding their order. Indians in French India were to remain Indian.

Another attempt was made to standardize citizenship and de-prioritize caste across the territories in 1872, when the government conferred the right to vote on Indians 'who have been exercising their trade on our territory for several years, or whose family live here or who own personal properties'. Once again they recognized locals for their tenure in the territory, either by domicile or by profession, but colonial sceptics and anti-assimilationists were uncomfortable by this precedent: the British hadn't allowed this, and what if other French colonies elsewhere suddenly began demanding similar rights? The then Governor General of French India, Antoine-Léonce Michaux, was worried that democracy and elections 'would end in reconstituting the Brahmanic social system and in giving it back its political influence that the Europeans have reduced but not destroyed'.

89

What followed in 1881 was the precursor to the law that, over time, has led to stories like Rajendran's. To address Pondicherry's divided society, the French instated a new rule by which Indians could come under French civil code if they renounced their personal status as natives. In becoming a 'renonçant', an individual gave up their caste and adopted a French 'nom', or family name. This decision was 'definitive and irrevocable for the renonçant himself as well as for his family and his descendants'.

Over the phone from Oslo, Ari Gautier of *The Hindu* fame delineates his family tree in some detail.

It started with his grandfather, who was a renonçant. 'He became Saminadin Gautier.' Spelt the French way, it is pronounced 'Saaminaathan'.

Gautier's description of how his grandfather and other renonçants acquired new names is the equivalent of someone going to a tailor, not being asked for any measurements, and returning with an ill-fitting suit. They would go to the Mayor's Office, La Mairie, sit across from a stranger and simply be given a new name. 'We used to joke that they had a French name calendar for every day of the year, hung up in the Mairie. So after giving out those 365 names, they just made up names for the rest. I know people named Chemise, Lenoir, Cordonnier'—shirt, black, and shoemaker. 'I'm sure the guy sitting on the other side of the desk was having a good time.'

The next significant renunciation was in 1947, when India emerged as its own independent nation: no longer British, no longer a colony. Political and demographic jolts followed in the 1950s, as the country's Portuguese and French pockets became restless. Historian and scholar William F. S. Miles dubs the next decade '[o]ne of the most unfortunate decolonizing experiences (at least from the French point of view)...a process which began in 1949, came to a crest in 1954, but was finalized only in 1962'.

What began in 1949 was a referendum all the way up in Bengal, in Chandernagore, French India's northern-most comptoir. The people overwhelmingly voted to merge with India. Reeling from the loss, the French described the outcome as 'le grand démantèlement', or 'the great dismantling', of their empire abroad. After this, they were reluctant to relinquish control of any of their southern enclaves, but the Indian government, now an actual entity, exerted pressure on the French to do just that. In 1954 they imposed sanctions on the French enclaves and restricted movement between them.

On 1 November 1954, a date known as the de facto transfer day, Pondicherry officially joined the Union of India. But the French took two more years to draft their 'Traité de Cession', or Transfer Treaty of 1956, and another five years to ratify it. By the time the French had fully handed over control to the Indian union, it was 16 August 1962, referred to as the de jure date of transfer.

During this time, the French were wondering how best to hold on to the citizens they had cultivated in India. The Treaty of Cession of the Territory of the Free City of Chandernagore, approved in 1951 and ratified in 1952, had automatically made those living in 'la Ville Libre' nationals and citizens of India. Residents could opt for—that is, retain—French citizenship, but very few did, based on records from the time, as well as how seamlessly the town was absorbed into West Bengal. Miles writes: 'Its autonomous status as a "Free City"... was thereby undone. Administratively, Chandernagore became an undifferentiated part of wider West Bengal, with no legal or administrative peculiarity to mark its previous status as a French possession.'

Perhaps 'undone', but not yet outdone, the French looked to their much larger and more settled establishment in the south for the loyalty they had lost in Chandernagore. Weary of losing even more citizens to India, they drafted their next transfer treaty with additional clauses about conserving and adopting nationality based on birthplace 'in the territory of the Establishments and domiciled therein'. This created a doubling of French nationals: those who migrated to France after the transfer, as the government expected, and those who chose to stay on in Pondicherry, building a French–Indian population that 'would multiply and prosper as an alien community'. The consequences, Miles points out, have created 'loophole[s] haunting French consular officials in Pondicherry today': people line up at the consulate to demand, or beg for, their allegedly legal right to migrate to France over fifty years after the treaty's conditions have expired.

÷

Historian Claude Arpi argues that the hastily written treaty resulted in decades-long waits for visas and 'le joli passeport bleu'—back when the French passport was in fact blue in colour. He writes that it was prepared without 'l'attention necessaire'. As a result, and to no one's surprise, the document had several 'lacunes'.

In 2004, Arpi compiled a retrospective subtitled 'L'intégration des Établissements Français en Inde' (the Integration of French Settlements in India). The booklet celebrates fifty years of Pondicherry's transfer from French to Indian rule. It contains 'perspectives historiques et culturelles' penned by ambassadors from France and from India, French travellers from the mid-twentieth century, correspondence between Prime Minister Nehru and his British counterparts, interviews with prominent locals, and more.

Helpfully, Arpi devotes several pages to an explanation of the Traité de Cession by Former Madras High Court Justice David Annoussamy. His 'remarquable exposition' explains how the 1956 Treaty guaranteed citizens an option to preserve or switch to the nationality of their choice, but then obfuscated how this was actually to be done. Citizens were allowed six months to exercise this choice, but were not given clear guidelines to follow. The text of the transfer was first printed in newspapers in 1956, 'sans grande pompe', without much ceremony, but not republished after 1962, the de jure transfer date, at which point the six-month window kicked off. Instead, there was a notice posted in the consulate, and the rest of the information dissemination through the city was left to word of mouth. Those who were Frenchified enough to be aware of the new policies exercised 'l'option', as it became known. In an ironic echo of caste tensions from 1819, early converts to French nationality kept l'option a secret from friends, colleagues, and even family members, so that the club remained exclusive.

They were aware of what to do, and by when; their rural and remote counterparts, however, were not.

But even if these people knowingly withheld the rules of l'option from non-elite Pondicherry society, they could not correctly anticipate who would jump at the opportunity to travel abroad and who would prefer to continue in India. Not everyone, Annoussamy points out, was interested in leaving India to 'aller chercher fortune', to try their luck in France. Political and business families, for example, retained Indian citizenship as a matter of pride, and because they were doing just fine where they were.

Indrani Singh Cassime notes that her father-in-law, C. M. Achraff, retained Indian citizenship for political reasons, whereas some of his siblings are French. She compares his family's decisions to adopt a certain citizenship to the question of buying a plot of land somewhere. 'It was just a normal thing then; it's become quite a big deal now.' Affluent Muslims are not desperate to become French citizens, she says. In the Muslim Quarter, 'within these three-four lanes, the Muslims are well-to-do. They own property, have big houses; there [in France] they might not be owning anything. My nieces and nephews aren't interested [in moving abroad]. They think it's a better life here.'

There were three main groups of people who took l'option, Annoussamy explains: retirees of the state and their families; civil servants and those in the military who were serving abroad and preferred to stay there;

and certain low caste communities who believed they would receive better treatment outside India's prejudiced borders. Many in this last group came from families who had become renonçants back in 1881, converted to Catholicism, and exercised l'option to protect their French nationality. Today, several of these citizens are retired and happily settled back in Pondicherry, such as Monsieur and Madame Dragon, where their foreign pensions supersede caste hierarchies. As Banik illustrated while walking me past the Dragons' home, their church is the largest, their evening pétanque game the most prominent in the city, and their patriotism unquestioned every 14 July, when they sing 'La Marseillaise' under the blazing summer heat.

In its bid to curate who would adopt which citizenship, the treaty's stipulations about marriage, children, and domicile further clashed with the South Indian Tamil-influenced traditions practised by its locals. As far as Hindus were concerned, for example, marriage had to be within the same caste, which forced Pondicherry men to travel as far as necessary to find a suitable wife, disrupting domicile rules. Children were traditionally born in the mother's parents' home, which affected their nationality. And a child accidentally omitted from the father's legal declaration, or unaware of the choice they had to make at age eighteen when l'option became active, could end up with a nationality different from their father's, effectively chopping off a branch of the family tree. Indian doctors who trained at the French hospitals in France or in Pondicherry lost their equivalent licence in France, and those who did not adopt French nationality were, 'all of a sudden, considered to be in a separate category. Abandoned by [the] French and not recognized by Indians.' Dr Nallam V., a renowned doctor in Pondicherry, and recognized by Pondicherry's medical community and diaspora alike, wrote *History of Medicine in French India* in 2014 to mourn the 'history and the contribution of these French trained doctors, who now belong to a category in a process of disappearance'.

Gautier annotates this 'disturbing process' over the phone in rapid, candid English. The 1962 laws, he argues, were 'so badly communicated to the people that most didn't understand them. My father was French, and my uncle—his own brother—was Indian. My father speaks French and worked in the French army. My uncle cannot and did not. It wasn't clear that someone had to go through the option process, and when my uncle asked about what he should do to retain his father's nationality, he was told that he didn't have to do anything—which was wrong! He remained in India and managed to make a good life for himself, but the kind of injustice you can feel in families is immense.'

Families being separated by geography often meant that those abroad fared better financially than those in India. 'It happened a lot where one segment of the family became well to do, while the other—the brother, the cousins, whoever—begged at the door. The guy who hadn't taken l'option would not be allowed in; he'd just linger outside the house, sitting on the thinnai,' Gautier explains, referring to the front porch of traditional Tamil homes where passers-by, travelling farmers, and other businessmen would sit and interact with the men of the household, without disrupting the activity inside the house or accidentally encountering the women.

If Gautier lived in Pondicherry today, his would be a coveted thinnai: 'My family lived inside the boulevards; my relatives living outside were considered Madrasi.' It's no coincidence that Gautier's immediate family was savvy enough to exercise l'option correctly and in time, unlike his extended family who were far beyond the boulevard's protective embrace. The Franco–Pondicherrian community had 'grown sceptical of the non-French. They practiced a very strict endogamy' that the Transfer Treaty exacerbated after 1962.

97

Proving the right kind of residence in the right parts of the union territory could mean a one-way ticket to France. This led to a proliferation of le 'résidence fictive', or fictitious residences, both in France and in Pondicherry. In fact, recent applications for French visas and passports have been based on false and 'fictive' documentation. Families in Pondicherry have stolen death certificates of actual French citizens and appropriated them into their family, says one tourism official who was hired as part of an investigative team from Delhi to verify the applications flooding the embassy. He has visited several families to interview them about their background, and observed that certain members—typically the older ones—are asked to keep silent so that the younger relatives can do the talking. When he speaks to the elders, he is not surprised to find that their family details do not match, or that the documents they proffer look obviously forged. People will do anything to leave, he says, they have a 'craze' for France. Being Pondichérien means being French, so people want to live there.

Gautier agrees. 'Someone who has not done l'option will try every possible way to go to France,' he says. Asked about Rajendran, he recalls, 'Rajendran is my step-cousin. His grandfather was a cook for the French. He was promised citizenship, but it never happened.'

98

÷

When Nehru visited Pondicherry on 16 January 1955 to welcome the union territory into India's fold, he was optimistic about an Indo–French alliance. 'While Pondicherry may be a small, very small part of India,' he said in a speech to Mayor Muthu Pillai and a gathered audience, 'it is a symbol of many things. It has now become a symbol of this friendly solution by negotiated settlement between nations of problems that troubled them. Therefore, this settlement truly brought joy and happiness to me.'

As part of his visit, Nehru was invited to a lunch hosted by M. Ramamurti, my great-grandfather and the then head of UCO Bank, which had recently taken over the regal Bank of Indochine building on one side of Bharati Park. His daughter, R. Devanayaki, remembers that government officials had asked if lunch could be held there 'as it was grand and a big place, which could accommodate many'. Ramamurti agreed.

Back then the branch manager's family lived on the first floor, above the bank, as they do today; the European layout still retains the large rooms, high ceilings, tall windows and complicated plumbing and wiring. In the fifties, food was prepared in a basement kitchen and sent upstairs in a dumb waiter, which, today, no longer works. Hosting lunch, Devanayaki explains, meant sharing part of their home with the guests. 'Two rooms—the drawing and the dining—were given to them,' she recalls.

Ramamurti and his wife formally received Nehru, Indira Gandhi and the then finance minister, T. T. Krishnamachari. Ramamurti's granddaughter Meenakshi was part of the welcome committee as 'Nehru liked kids'. Then lunch was served. 'A huge feast was prepared outside as it included non-vegetarian [food], and was served separately to a huge number of people.' Meanwhile, the family 'was kept in the pantry and given rasam saadam!' she says. 'We were not allowed to meet [the guests] due to security reasons, but we peeped at them from somewhere!'

÷

Nehru wanted Pondicherry to 'continue to be a seat in

many ways of the French language'. In earlier remarks made on 27 August 1947, he had lamented that '[w]e have looked at the world through British spectacles for too long. We want our youth to acquire a more universal intellectual training that only French culture can give us.'

But seventy years later, Virapattiname Balaya and Raymond Saravanin, ambassadors in their own right, have reservations about what French culture has to offer. After serving in the French Army for over twenty years, they returned to a Pondicherry they found much changed. The streets are too crowded, they complain, and what was once farmland has been covered with buildings. The Manakula Vinayagar Temple has grown large and noisy. The boys and girls are far less disciplined than they remember, and the women drink and smoke, which, they exclaim, is 'aberrant' and 'degoutant', disgusting!

Now retired, their wives equally at leisure, their children grown and settled abroad, these former soldats keep busy in a building dedicated to them. A bright yellow structure in the French Quarter with the tricolour flying at full mast, it stands just a few blocks from the beach. Above the tall front door is a three-coloured sign, 'FOYER DU SOLDAT', which translates to 'the soldier's home'. The two veterans explain that the premises costs a symbolic ₹12 in rent and was renovated in 2011 for ₹80 lakh. A room is ₹3,000 per night; accommodation is only for the military and for French citizens. It is a short commute for Balaya and Saravanin, who live just outside the boulevards, near its northern edge. 'Inside the boulevard are mostly old families,' Balaya says, underscoring the very policies that created soldats in the first place.

At sixty-two, his white-flecked eyebrows contrast with his dark skin. His deep voice overpowers the small room; 'personellement,' he begins—'personally'—and his colleague knows to stop talking. Saravanin, older by ten years, is quieter. Perhaps there is a correlation with their professions; Saravanin was in the navy. Balaya was a parachutist.

Inside the manager's office, the lighting is dim and the ceiling fan whirs loudly. The men sit at separate desks arranged in an L-shape and wait patiently for my phone recorder to turn on. They are happy to be answering questions from an 'académique' rather than a reporter who might misrepresent their words.

During the Transfer of 1962, both men were teenagers and took l'option through their fathers for French citizenship. They joined the army and were posted in a number of French colonies, from Guadeloupe to Martinique, from French Polynesia to Haiti, from Senegal to Gabon. Then they settled in France, where they got married to women who themselves had migrated from Pondicherry through their fathers; community was important to these men. Eventually they returned to Pondicherry for reasons ranging from property, language and climate, to a certain facet of

Indian culture: respect for parents. Discovering that youth here are as liberated as those in France, however, did not reconcile with their memories of the quiet town they had grown up in.

Unlike some of their retired friends, they are not religious—not in the conventional sense. Saravanin believes in a God that lives within, and Balaya does not wish to thoughtlessly follow religious leaders. He has never been to Sri Aurobindo Ashram Samadhi. Rather, he booms in perfect French, 'I believe in my parents: if they weren't here I wouldn't be here; true or false?' Neither sees a need to judge the Ashram or its pan-Indian allure. 'They speak French. It's there; that's fine.'

Without work or religion to attend to, how do they spend their time? Balaya picks up a stack of papers from his desk and reads aloud from the printed itinerary on top. It's the schedule for the upcoming Bastille Day festivities on 14 July, which include a military parade. They are keen to use fireworks. 'All are welcome,' Balaya announces, as if speaking to an imaginary crowd. Being French citizens, they cannot vote in Pondicherry, but the 'Nehru treaty'—referring to the Transfer Treaty of 1956—allows them to do everything else. And they are easily able to keep up with city politics; an old friend and former classmate is now chief minster, and they meet him regularly.

Nehru had envisioned Pondicherry as a 'fenêtre ouverte sur la France', an open window into France. Balaya and Saravanin, having spent time on both sides of this window, are ultimately content to spend the autumn of their lives where they spent the spring. But they understand the excitement of travelling outside India, and experiencing life elsewhere. 'The locals here believe it is good in France,' Balaya says. 'Ils aiment déplacer,' they would like to move there. But 'la vie est dure'—life there is hard, too.

Not for Rajendran, whose lack of daily routine in Pondicherry bores him. Nor for the families who have co-opted deceased strangers as ancestors to prove their legal French status. Nor the long queues of hopefuls at the consulate, who have memorized every detail of the French citizen they are about to marry. 'C'est la vie,' the saying goes: that's life, and there isn't much one can do about it. But *ma* vie, *my* life; that's worth having l'option to control and make decisions about for as long as possible.

103

SEVEN

A Supramental Life

As the queues for French visas grow longer, I am struck by the nearly hundred-year-old immigration *into* Pondicherry whose cause and effect can be explained in two words: Sri Aurobindo. This city—small, segregated, multi-cultural, Tamil—is also home to one of India's best known and internationally recognizable ashrams. In existence since 1928, today it has about 2,000 members living in Pondicherry. Several buildings in White Town and others dotted throughout the rest of the city are Ashram properties, identified by the twelve-petalled flower carved into their gates and doors, or the photos of Sri Aurobindo and the Mother framed and hung visibly in the entrances of homes, hotel rooms and restaurants. Both of them preached about the 'supramental', a divine consciousness that, once established in people's minds, would bring about ideal, harmonious communities of living. These words are often heard in the Ashram community today.

The choice of Pondicherry for an ashram was an accident of circumstance. At the turn of the twentieth century, before he was any kind of guru, Aurobindo

Ghose was someone else entirely: a Cambridge-returned Bengali keeping busy in British India—in Calcutta and Baroda—with various projects. He conducted political studies, tutored privately, immersed himself in Sanskrit and other classical Indian texts—all the while following and supporting anti-colonial activity in India and other parts of the world, and intermittently spending time in jail because of it. Before 1910, Ghose's activities had earned him the reputation of a revolutionary in British India who needed to be contained. Restless, he escaped Calcutta for Chandernagore and then decided to undertake a much longer journey to an even quieter, even more distant French territory in South India. Ghose was tiring of purely political campaigns; he sought transformation at a deeper, more personal level. Pondicherry, he had heard, could provide the quiet he needed to focus on his sadhana, or yogic practice.

On 4 April 1910, Ghose arrived in Pondicherry and stayed hidden while British warrants for his arrest waited for him in the larger cities. He engaged in long discussions with Subramania Bharati, also in hiding from the British, also a poet and thinker. Ghose was prolific, and started the *Arya* magazine in 1914 to practise articulating his own philosophical thoughts and questions. One biography notes that over the next six years he published 'some 4,600 pages of philosophy, commentary, translations, and essays in *Arya*; composed a verse play and a long narrative poem; filled two dozen notebooks with translations, commentaries, and notes on the Vedas; wrote diary entries equal in length to a nine-hundred-page book; and corresponded with several associates'.

People all over India, but mostly Ghose's fellow Bengalis, had begun hearing about this man and his spiritual ideology. They travelled long distances to meet him, and many never left Pondicherry after. In 1922, a French woman named Blanche Rachel Mirra Alfassa moved in with Ghose. She and her husband Paul Richards were spiritually inclined and developed a close relationship with Ghose. Alfassa became Ghose's primary student, which Richards took time to adjust to. But Ghose was uninterested in the social and personal implications of his partnership with Mirra, or Mira, or Sri Mira Devi, as he called her. It wasn't long before Richards left India for good, alone.

In November 1926, Ghose underwent a transformation, which he transcribed as 'an oceanic flood of Light rushing down from above. Everyone present felt a kind of pressure above his head. The whole atmosphere was surcharged with some electrical energy.' Although Ghose did not speak about this event for nearly a decade, Mirra declared to one devotee that '"the Ananda" or plane of cosmic bliss had "descended in the physical."' By the end of 1926, Ghose had become 'Sri Aurobindo' to his devotees, or sadhaks.

Immediately after this experience, Sri Aurobindo entrusted Mirra with leadership of his devotees: 'Mirra is my Shakti. She has taken charge of the new creation.

You will get everything from her. Give [your] consent to whatever she wants to do.' As Ghose's new title became more established in the community, the sadhaks followed Sri Aurobindo's example and began addressing Sri Mira Devi as the Mother. By the end of 1928, within twenty years of Ghose's arrival in Pondicherry, the tiny community of some fifteen houses became known as the Ashram.

Re-enter Peter Heehs, of morning jogs and Bharati Park stories. He moved to Pondicherry in 1971 and joined the Ashram to slake his spiritual thirst. While he was one of the main editors at the Sri Aurobindo Ashram Archives, Heehs studied and catalogued all kinds of material, including the writings of Sri Aurobindo and the Mother. He explains that the Mother began buying plots of land as the Ashram received monetary donations, and eventually a lot of White Town became Ashram property. Today that land is worth multiple times what she would have paid. 'The Mother bought at a good time,' Heehs says.

Another long-time resident muses about the growth of Pondicherry the city, and Pondicherry the Ashram. Comparing it to Cuddalore, she says, 'I suppose Cuddalore has grown at the same pace as Pondicherry, but it could be any place in Tamil Nadu; Pondicherry is distinct in many respects. There's certainly a presence— atmosphere or pretence, depends on how you want to look at it.'

÷

In a letter written to a devotee in 1933, twenty-three years after he had arrived in Pondicherry, Sri Aurobindo explained the word 'supramental':

> What the supramental will do the mind cannot foresee or lay down. The mind is ignorance seeking for the Truth, the supramental by its very definition is the Truth-Consciousness. Truth in possession of itself and fulfilling itself by its own power. In a supramental world imperfection and disharmony are bound to disappear. But what we propose just now is not to make the earth a supramental world but to bring down the supramental as a power and established consciousness in the midst of the rest—to let it work there and fulfil itself as Mind descended into Life and Matter and has worked as a Power there to fulfil itself in the midst of the rest. This will be enough to change the world and to change Nature by breaking down her present limits. But what, how, by what degrees it will do it, is a thing that ought not to be said now—when the Light is there, the Light will itself do its work— when the supramental Will stands on earth, that Will will decide. It will establish a perfection, a harmony, a Truth-creation—for the rest, well, it will be the rest—that is all.

Pondicherry was growing restless under French rule in the 1930s and 1940s, and crowds had started gathering around Sri Aurobindo to hear his wisdom. He shared this sparingly, when he was not doing meditation, writing political and spiritual essays, or holding private discussions. 'One has to pass beyond and supramentalise overmind so that mind and all the rest may undergo the final change,' he wrote cryptically in a letter in 1933. Two years later he wrote that that the 'overmind' had descended, which he defined as 'a transitional plane between mind and supermind. Its "descent", that is, its manifestation in the physical world, was necessary before the supermind could itself descend.' By 1937, Sri Aurobindo devotees numbered 200, primarily from Bengal and Orissa in India, and from the UK and France in the West. Construction to house them was spreading through White Town.

In the late 1940s, Sri Aurobindo's revised and collected chapters of an earlier book, *The Life Divine*, was published in the US. Western readers then flocked to Pondicherry to meet this profound and unique thinker, by which point crowds in the thousands would gather outside the Ashram for a glimpse of Sri Aurobindo and the Mother. Although Sri Aurobindo passed away on 5 December 1950, it is said that his body was kept on view for nearly five days before any decomposition began to show. The Mother observed an 'aura of light around the body', as did some of the journalists who wrote about the sage's passing, cementing in many devotees' minds the fact that Sri Aurobindo had brought a certain light to mankind, to society, to their Ashram in Pondicherry. Considering the number of people who continue to visit the Ashram every year, even seventy years later, I marvel at the strength of his radiance and philosophy.

÷

Some of Sri Aurobindo's oldest devotees are today in their eighties, bright eyed and sprightly. They came to Pondicherry as young children in the 1940s and chose never to leave. Asked how the Ashram has changed in nearly a century, one septuagenarian points out that his generation, unlike the ones that came after, personally knew Sri Aurobindo and the Mother. 'People here are devoted; they are not devotees.' Individuals, then couples, and then families arrived from all over North India, travelling in the 1940s when cross-country migration required totally uprooting and journeying for weeks. Sri Aurobindo and the Mother were prepared for this kind of dedication in their followers, but that their followers would come with children, who needed somewhere to go while their parents were serving, studying, meditating—that presented a new challenge. Once the Mother realized that devotees were travelling with children, and that children needed a school, a new dimension of the Ashram was established. And some of its first students, Kittu Reddy, Urmila Patel, Lata Jauhar—referred to throughout the Ashram by their first names and the Bengali suffixes da and di—are still involved with the school today, as teachers, mentors and administrators. One school principal remembers how he began teaching at the school decades ago, without any conventional qualifications: 'One day I was a student; the next day I was a teacher.'

This was the same for eighty-six-year-old Lata Jauhar, better known as Lata di, who moved to Pondicherry from Delhi when she was twelve years old. Just about five feet tall, she is immediately recognizable when she walks through the town, erect and without a cane, in long floral-printed dresses that come down to her ankles. She teaches French in the Ashram school using the Mother's prayers, and Spanish using pop songs that her students have meticulously copied into their notebooks. While the former might seem more serious, the latter conveys its own life philosophies of love, melody and rhythm—Lata di makes sure of that.

From a large and wealthy family, she is one of several Jauhars who keeps the Ashram humming. Her younger sister, eighty-one, manages the Sri Aurobindo Ashram Delhi branch operations, including admissions to Mother's International, one of the capital's most selective schools. While its values originate from the teachings of Sri Aurobindo and the Mother, the Delhi school is distinctly more urban, hectic, and competitive. Another Jauhar sister keeps equally busy running the Ashram farm some kilometres outside of Pondicherry. She drives to and from the city twice a day with fresh dairy and produce, and otherwise keeps to herself. 'Talk

111

to my sister,' she says, barely looking over her shoulder as she unloads vegetables from her car. 'I don't like to talk to people.'

Luckily for me, Lata di is the opposite. Walking through White Town with her feels like walking with the president of the country: she is constantly nodding, smiling, waving at former students, and can recall their names and the names of their children, whom she has likely also taught. They wave back from their bicycles and mopeds, young girls looking like young boys in their crisp sports uniforms, their hair wrapped in white head cloths, not out of modesty but for easy physical movement during games. Because of the Mother, women and girls were wearing shorts in Pondicherry decades before the rest of the country tolerated it. Lata di has photos of herself as a young girl wearing that same uniform.

She identifies houses that have been torn down, rebuilt, made taller, or divided into apartments. Here is her family home in Pondicherry; next to it is her sister's produce shed; across the street is where her late brother used to live; and a few blocks closer to the Ashram headquarters is the guest house where she spends the day before retiring to her family home to sleep. The keys to each of these places jingle in her bag. Walking past the Delhi Branch Guest House, reserved for ashramites visiting from Delhi, Lata di offers it to to me as a lodging option. 'Stay here next time; I have the keys,' she says nonchalantly, and laughs at the suggestion that she is Pondicherry's best connected apartment broker. This reveals her toothless smile, which provokes more life philosophy: 'An Italian friend kept telling me to get dentures, but I refused.' As a result she misses the taste of peanuts, but 'you don't have to eat everything'.

Her close friend Urmila di is similarly practical. Hard of hearing and uncomfortable wearing a hearing aid, she only keeps it on for an hour on Sunday afternoons to receive phone calls from loved ones. The rest of the week she only communicates with whomever is available in person, and is perfectly content doing so. Habituated to daily exercise from her days as a student of the Ashram—a sixty-year-old routine—she continues her evening callisthenics in the sports ground on the beach. She lives on the northern side of the Manakula Vinayagar Temple, where the road is forever congested because of locals parking their new cars there for pujas. Despite the crowds and shops just outside her front gate, her home is absolutely peaceful. Each of the rooms is small and full of books, with ceiling-high, curtain-less windows to allow ventilation, with no attempt at privacy. 'You are in the Ashram, so you have no social life; your focus must be on your work,' Urmila di says, introducing her home with a slow sweep of her wrinkled arm. But the hallway is long, bright, and uncluttered. Sunlight streams into an inner courtyard, greeting four tall potted plants. Large framed photos of Sri Aurobindo and the Mother peer down from different walls, as if locked in conversation with the flora. 'My father designed this house with such care. The outside is inside, so I never feel lonely.'

Ashramites are constantly negotiating the outside and the inside, whether their school grounds, the city of Pondicherry, their national borders, or, most intangibly, their own consciousness. Two former students of Lata di, now grown men with families, have seen the world, studied or sent children abroad, but they are most excited to keep up their local routine: a twice-daily cigarette-and-cutting-chai break on Canal Road, which is a two-way road running on either side of the canal. 'Don't tell anyone!' they say to me, before proceeding to exchange local gossip: the salt residue collecting on their windows; a new history book about Pondicherry; family updates. The pillion seat of their motorcycles is ever ready for passengers, whether to drop Lata di home, or to escort a curious tourist to the Catholic church opposite the railway station. One of them has been teaching history at the Ashram school for a few months, and perks up at the names of new historical biography titles. 'I'm on the lookout for a good textbook, like what they have in America,' he says, in between sips of his hot, sugary tea. 'Don't tell them this, but I teach outside of the Mother and Sri Aurobindo. I want to look at history in depth and with focus.'

In *The Ideal of Human Unity*, which Sri Aurobindo first published in 1919 and revised a few times until 1950, he argues that '[h]istory teaches us nothing; it is a confused torrent of events and personalities or a kaleidoscope of changing institutions'. This, along with the Mother's instincts for raising happy children, has brought about one of India's more liberated alternative education systems, the Sri Aurobindo International Centre of Education (SAICE), located a few blocks from the Ashram. Known as the Ashram School, its students do not graduate from one grade to the next, nor do they take exams, follow set syllabi or collect transcripts at the end of their tenure. Instead, they choose their subjects, including independent projects, from the time they are fourteen or fifteen, and spend as much time building aquariums and singing Spanish songs as they do analysing Sri Aurobindo's poetry or climate-friendly urban architecture. Instruction is in English as well as French. The students learn from practitioners, travellers, devotees, teachers who love learning as much as they do. Theirs is an education of passion that bursts open as a bud into a flower. Since every student has the privilege of unhurriedly exploring their own interests, they take their time moving through texts, ideas, and discussions.

Debabrata Sahoo—known as Debo—is an alumnus of the school, now in his thirties, who regularly visits the school dorms to check up on the younger students and accompany them on field trips. But he is rarely spotted at the Ashram meditation sites. 'I carry the Ashram and Matrimandir in my heart,' he says, referring to the most sacred structure of the community, located 20 kilometres away in Auroville. He confesses that he prefers scuba diving with his teachers to sitting with them in a classroom. 'They teach you how to learn. You learn to learn. I would just stare out the window. Knowledge is by the sea.'

Everything an ashramite expresses carries multiple layers of meaning. It is not surprising to encounter students and former students who still remember the prayers and poetry they learned in school, who code-switch between English, French and a range of Indian languages to communicate a school memory. Like Urmila di's house and Debo's weekend diving trips, the different atmospheres in which learning takes place blend together: neither purely inside a classroom nor outside the campus; neither by the wisdom of elders nor by the spunk and spontaneity of self-driven study. Like Lata di's and Kittu da's transformation from student to teacher, the process of meditating upon an idea follows instinct rather than logic. In Sri Aurobindo's words: 'Ideas sometimes leap out as armed forces and break their way through the hedge of unideal powers.'

÷

If ideas can wage war, perhaps it is not surprising when the consequences are correspondingly bloody. In 2008, Heehs wrote a book about his guru, *The Lives of Sri Aurobindo,* published by Columbia University Press. But a subset of the community took great offence to his project and its thorough, deliberate investigation into Aurobindo's life. They filed a case in the Orissa

High Court to ban the book, arguing that Heehs had depicted Sri Aurobindo as a man and not an idol, and that *The Lives* 'contains matters which are deliberately and maliciously intended to insult the religious beliefs of millions of Indians who idolize Sri Aurobindo as a National Hero and incarnation of "Almighty"'. They said that its publication had 'sent shock waves throughout the community of thousands of devotees and disciples of Sri Aurobindo'.

In December 2008, the central government directed the state government of Delhi and the union government in Pondicherry 'to ensure that there should be no publication of the objectionable book without obtaining a no objection from the Government of India'—practically banning it throughout the country. Similarly, the Government of Orissa ordered that 'every copy of the objectionable book, its copies, reprints, translations, or other documents containing extracts taken therefrom...[be] forfeited to the Government'. Heehs was also stripped of his access to the Ashram Archives, and became the target of several fiery letters and accusations written by other Ashram devotees.

Although not in print in India, *The Lives* is available on the Internet as excerpts on Amazon.com and Google Books, and in its entirety on a Russian-hosted website titled 'Site of Sri Aurobindo & The Mother'. On the Columbia University Press blog, Heehs explains that only a kaleidoscopic survey of the multi-faceted, British-educated, Independence-aspiring, yoga-practising

Aurobindo could have done justice to the man himself:

> The Aurobindo that interests me is the one who
> turned from a life of hectic action to a life of
> contemplation, but was able, during his forty-
> year retirement, to write a shelf full of books on
> philosophy, political theory, and textual criticism,
> along with thousands of letters and, yes, that epic
> in iambic pentameter. People will continue to
> differ about the significance of his work, but its
> very mass is there for all to see. His life as a yogi
> and spiritual leader is more difficult to quantify,
> but it certainly will not be forgotten soon. I tried
> to do justice to all sides of this versatile man,
> but to do so I had to be unconventional in more
> ways than one.

The response to his book was unconventional too: while one group of devotees revolted against the book and demanded that severe action be taken against its author, the Ashram Trustees refused to expel Heehs from their community altogether. Instead they assisted Heehs in renewing his visa, and allowed him to stay on in Ashram accommodations. There was resistance, but also a kind of tolerance. Today, eleven years after writing *The Lives*, Heehs still lives here and continues to work with archival material, just not Sri Aurobindo's. He has survived the release of his next book, *Writing the Self*, which came out in 2013, *Writing the Self*, and examines Christian thought during the Renaissance.

118

But the Ashram community's unhappiness at Heehs's biography has endured since 2008, and even today his name is hardly whispered in the Ashram Archives. Large and flower-scented, the Archives building on Nehru Street lies behind unobtrusive wooden doors. The latch doesn't always catch, so I make sure to carefully re-close the door and turn the doorknob a few times on my way in. Stepping into the courtyard is to be greeted by thriving flowering plants and bushes, a bicycle parked in one corner, and open doors that lead into the senior archivists' offices. Up a narrow flight of stairs in the back is a landing that opens onto three book-filled rooms, one kitchen, and the terrace. Indoors or outdoors, the air is silent, rich with the smell and texture of books, letters, papers and folders that are neatly stacked, categorized, labelled. Everything seems to be in a state of mid-contemplation: a new translation of something Sri Aurobindo or the Mother wrote, perhaps, or an edited volume of articles by Sri Aurobindo scholars that is to be published soon.

119

Heehs' presence—or is it his absence—is still felt amidst the papers, books, and potted plants. One of his colleagues, a tall, laconic scholar named Bob offers me the spare desk, offhandedly alluding to the person who used to sit there before he was 'cruelly pushed out'. Besides that, Bob does not mention Heehs. He hardly speaks at all, in fact, except to laugh wryly at a joke, or locate an article. When I let slip that I know where the spare key to the Archives office is hidden, his eyes twinkle.

Like the spare key, the mystical secrets of the Ashram are hidden in plain sight. Sri Aurobindo's and the Mother's writings have been translated into different languages, published as lengthy volumes and bite-sized daily thoughts. Disciples can meditate in Sri Aurobindo's old room and eat three meals under enormous framed portraits of the Mother and Sri Aurobindo. Everywhere one looks within the boulevards of Pondicherry, there is a building painted the muted grey and white colours of the Ashram, its nameplate often in the Mother's handwriting and advertising a unique business—Senteurs, where they manufacture perfumes; or the Embroidery Department office. The Ashram buildings and businesses are themselves a microcosm of Pondicherry's most alluring sites: the Samadhi, where Sri Aurobindo and the Mother are buried; the dining hall; the school; the college; the main library; the Marbling and Hand Printed Paper factories; the Exhibition House gallery on the Promenade; the guest houses; the Ashram devotee lodgings and sunny playground; the sports grounds; the dairy; the grain distribution centre; Honesty, the grocery store. Each of these institutions, private homes, guest houses and even autorickshaws wear four eyes on their walls, Sri Aurobindo's and the Mother's, so that all activities are supervised by and dedicated to them.

Indeed, the 2,000-odd full-time ashramites living in Pondicherry and working in these various establishments do not earn any money for their services; rather, they are provided for by the Sri Aurobindo Ashram Trust, which administers the Ashram and awards 'Prosperity' to ashramites every month, described on the Ashram website as 'clothes, toiletries and other necessary commodities'. The trust is managed by a board of five trustees and oversees about eighty Ashram-run departments 'which include farms, gardens, healthcare, guesthouses and engineering units among many others'. Several of these departments engage in commercial activity in Pondicherry, through which income and profit is made. But the Ashram's revenue mostly comes from donations and the ashramites who, when they become members, hand over all their private wealth and assets in a 'kind of spiritual obligation', although this is not required for people to become members of the Ashram.

121

The commercial activity is not insignificant. For many tourists, the Ashram experience means staying in a boutique hotel—more often a restored French building than a Tamil home—visiting the Samadhi, and purchasing lots of Sri Aurobindo and Auroville products. These range from books to incense sticks, from handmade paper to clothing, from accessories to perfume. While the Ashram dining hall food is simple and the guest houses spartan, their for-sale offerings are not nearly as unadorned. Like so many other spiritual communities, Sri Aurobindo Ashram has become another commodity, another politics.

But this does not seem to affect members of the

community, especially lifelong ones. 'For us, the whole of Pondicherry was an Ashram,' says Lata di. Sitting next to her is another chatty octogenarian, Vrinda di, originally from Maharashtra, her white hair in a thick braid. She shows off her hand-embroidered portraits of Sri Aurobindo and the Mother, placing their gazes at eye level this time. Both women, as well as Urmila di, hail from large and affluent families who gladly offered their belongings to the Ashram when they settled in Pondicherry over fifty years ago. Vrinda di blushes at compliments on her artwork, and dismisses any notion of technique, for she was never trained to draw or stitch. It's all there before you, she insists. 'Take a flower and a magnifying glass, look at it, and let it show you.'

122

Along with the flower symbol on gates and doors, the names of these homes or their residents quickly reveal that the tenants are ashramites. Auroposée is Vrinda di's daughter, and one of the first children to be born to an Ashram devotee. Aurodhan is an art gallery and performance space that buzzes every evening with cultural activity and owner Lalit Verma's stentorian voice and figure. These Auro-prefixed names evoke the Ashram's spiritual leadership, while buildings labelled 'Harmony' and 'Gratitude' espouse their principles. Still, the Ashram's reputation is that it keeps to itself in the city, its members rarely mingling with non-Ashram citizens. Few make an effort to learn Tamil, instead using the Bengali, Oriya and Hindi that most ashramites speak, and switching to French or English when needed.

Dilip Kapur, founder of leather goods manufacturer Hidesign, admits that language is a barrier between different parts of the city. 'You can very easily live in a parallel world' in Pondicherry, he says. 'I have people here who spend ten years in the company and speak no Tamil. And you can.' Kapur is more proactive, though. 'All my kids speak some Tamil. Good or bad, they do speak it. All said, I'm a Tamil Punjabi. Not a Punjabi Tamil. I would have greater loyalty to my Tamil side than my Punjabi side—but probably much greater loyalty to Auroville and the Ashram than either of those two.'

Kapur was a student at the Ashram school before he left for the US to finish high school and attend university. He returned to India after completing his doctoral degree, because his heart belonged in Pondicherry; not even an invitation from Louis Vuitton to set up a Hidesign office in Paris could pull him away. 'I don't know a town this size in India that is as cosmopolitan. There are very few in the world. That's what makes me come back here. It is very different in thought. I'm comfortable here.' He pauses as his assistant hands him a Strepsil and a glass of water. 'The fact is that the Tamil culture overall is an extremely tolerant culture.' According to Kapur, it is this local passiveness that has allowed the Ashram to thrive the way it has.

But not everyone is this optimistic. Prakash Nanwani, who has run a tailoring and retail business on Nehru Street for over thirty years, scoffs at the Ashram's

123

values. 'You move here, give up everything you have, then ask for food? Is that a way to live?' Mrinmoyee Majumdar, a young woman who came to Pondicherry 'for a pause' in 2015 and does art space therapy, rolls a cigarette while talking about the Ashram. She works carefully against the breeze, which blows in from the sea and past her table on Hotel Ajanta's rooftop, a popular Promenade eatery. Majumdar appreciates the Ashram's respect for 'labour as yoga' and the Ashram's 'exploration of material' in their quest to make paper, fragrances, fabric. But she feels cut off from the senior leadership, whom she dismisses as 'grumpy old Ashram men' who meet at Qualité (pronounced the French way, kaa-lee-thay), one of the local bars, every evening. The owl tattoo on her back dances as she brings the cigarette to her lips.

S. Tamil Sengolan, a young local businessman whose telecom office is some distance beyond the boulevards, finds the Ashram 'too secluded'. He has political aspirations, and feels that the Ashram is ideal for those who want to pursue the arts, but doesn't teach people about 'real society'. Its members live 'subtle, quiet lives' and are not interested in rising to prominence, or making a mark for themselves in the public sphere. By contrast, Sengolan embraces the grit and persistence a political career requires. A poster next to his desk reads: 'Everyone wants to change the world but no one wants to change.'

Ashram sceptics or not; Heehs disavowers or

not, few disagree that Sri Aurobindo underwent a monumental spiritual transformation during his forty years in Pondicherry. Pondicherrians are tactful, if tacit, about a certain supramental tug that emanates from their city, and that has brought people from all over the country and the world to their shores, to visit the Ashram and bask in its aura. Some attribute it to the fresh flowers and easy silence in the Ashram courtyard where Sri Aurobindo and the Mother are buried. Others to the discipline and mental purity of its devotees. And some recall the glow that shone out of Sri Aurobindo's body after he had breathed his last; they still feel its rays lingering upon their skin, mingling with the sun by day, and with the moon by night.

EIGHT

Inheritance

About 200 years before Sri Aurobindo escaped Bengal for South India, a shipload of Jesuit missionaries had fled from Siam and set up a seminary just 10 kilometres south of Pondicherry, in Arikamedu. Interestingly, locals tend to be better informed about these eighteenth-century ruins than they are about the Ashram, or even Aayi Mandapam. Is it because Arikamedu was the site of one of India's oldest trading ports with the Romans, dating back to the first century? Or perhaps because it has been written about by Indian, French and British archaeologists, as well as in the landmark first-century Greco-Roman historical text *Periplus of the Erythraean Sea*? The answer is much simpler: excavations from the ruins are permanently featured at the Pondicherry Museum in White Town.

But one can visit Arikamedu if one knows the right person to ask. Yuvaraj calls two local history and archaeology enthusiasts, Ramesh and Murali, for an informal tour. I am back on Yuvaraj's bike, and am surprised when he slows down about thirty minutes after leaving Pondicherry, when we are still on the main road and nowhere near anything resembling ruins. But Yuvaraj has spotted Ramesh and Murali waiting on their motorcycles where the highway splits into tributaries of narrow streets. They start moving and Yuvaraj follows them through winding paths to reach the ruins. In the midst of some grassy fields, barely enclosed by a fence or announced with proper signage, are tall brick-and-stone structures, pillars, walls and archways that were once a seminary in the late 1700s.

Equally attention-catching are four men in white who are just hanging around, waiting for us to leave so that they can spread out and enjoy their midday drink, as if on a historically-inspired picnic. Sadly, evidence of past 'picnics' is apparent on the sandy ground around the pillars: strewn bottles and shards of green glass that Ramesh and Murali have learned to distinguish from the first-century beads and pieces of glass dating back to Roman trading activity in this part of the world, long before the missionaries arrived. The archaeological fragments glint in the sunlight, the millions of cracks on their surfaces a catalogue of the centuries the glass has been exposed to the elements.

Ramesh thumps against the wall to demonstrate how strong and solid the bricks are; they've been standing for over two hundred years. Room dimensions are easily distinguishable, as is a wide gate in the rear through which my guides walk, stooping occasionally to pick up thousand-year-old debris. Some of their findings have been installed at the Pondicherry Museum alongside

127

discoveries from archaeological digs done in the 1940s by A. Aiyappan, the then Superintendent of the Government Museum in Madras, French archaeologists Jouveau Dubreuil and Jean-Marie Casal, and British archaeologist Mortimer Wheeler.

The backdrop to the ruins is typical rural South India: rows of palm trees, untended grass and weeds. The ground is sandy and dry until it becomes the banks of the Ariyankuppam River, and dives abruptly into the water, daring visitors to lean too far and fall in. The river babbles about the region's history, but in a language no one can decipher. Still, Ramesh and his team have uncovered ancient bricks on the banks, buried under the grass and shrubbery.

128

The Archaeological Survey of India (ASI) has documented eleven historical sites within the union territory, by city and by 'sub-circle', on paper and online, but the physical sites are less organized. Murali rattles off all the site and district names, lamenting that they are badly maintained and rarely visited. Arikamedu and Nagapattinam are excavations and the remaining nine are temples in Bahour, Tiruvandarkoil, Tirubhuvanai, Madagadipattu in Pondicherry district, two in Karaikal, one in Cuddalore, and one more in Nagapattinam. 'Inga nariya paravai irruku,' Murali says about the abundance of birds; 'the peacock generation is now so much developed.' Snakes, too, especially cobras. While underfunded, the sites are overgrown, providing ideal conditions for wildlife.

Even Arikamedu, just a short drive from Pondicherry, is poorly signposted and unwelcoming, especially for lone travellers and women. Murali hustles the group out of the enclosure because the men in white are growing restless. They announce themselves a few times, snapping the stands of their motorcycles, and shuffling their bags of food and drink. In response, the archaeological crew kick their motorcycle stands up, rev their engines, and drive away.

÷

Within the boulevards, words like 'conservation', 'heritage', and 'boutique' are tossed around easily, backed by private and government efforts. Apt for Pondicherry, the word 'heritage' has its origins in the French verb 'heriter', meaning to inherit. And 'boutique', today used for fashionable clothing stores and restored hotel properties, comes from the French word for a small store. Connotations have emerged over time, and Pondicherry's tourist economy relies on the city's French, Tamil, and Franco-Tamoul architecture being renovated into 'heritage buildings' and 'boutique properties'. But conservation isn't only physical. Scholars flock to Pondicherry's archives to resurrect intellectual pursuits that otherwise live only in the past. The beach Promenade is one of Pondicherry's more prominent restorations, carefully reconstructed by INTACH from 2009–2011, to evoke a colonial outpost that even the locals may not have lived through.

129

But despite how beautifully ships twinkle on the horizon, a murkier story swirls below the waves. As conservation has advanced onto the cityscape, so has degradation seeped into the water. The lengthy sandy beach no longer exists and today, no one can access the actual water for a feet-wetting or a dip.

'Everyone had their spot where they would go swimming,' recalls Sunaina Mandeen, settling into a chair inside Palais de Mahe, a heritage hotel near the southern boulevard of the city. She is a co-founder of Pondy Citizens' Action Network, or PondyCAN, which is 'committed to preserve and enhance the natural, social, cultural and spiritual environment' of Pondicherry. The organization has campaigned for and organized several sustainability projects throughout the city, from distribution of natural and urban resources to 'environmental awareness and civic consciousness'. Her curly black hair in a bun, eyes bright and hands constantly moving, Mandeen bubbles with ideas for new projects, ways to get children involved, and schemes the government should heed. 'You can't have the government alone or the people alone,' she says about city-wide, or beach-long sustainability. 'It has to be a collaboration.'

Mandeen's partners are, first and foremost, her PondyCAN co-founders who came together in 2007: Probir Banerjee and Aurofilio Schiavina. It's not surprising that they studied at the Ashram, given their commitment to preserving the natural environment around them. Their Ashram connection, in fact, is apparent even from their names: Probir's Bengali parents came to Pondicherry to study under Sri Aurobindo, and Aurofilio and Auralice—who headed a separate environmental education program—were, like Vrinda di's daughter, named by the Mother.

This team has grown over the past ten years to include concerned locals and youth, volunteers from all over the world, and experts in the form of environmentalists, engineers, filmmakers and urban planners, to name a few. They rotate through the office, which is located just outside the boulevards and, quite aptly, a few hundred yards from the fisherman's village in Kuruchikuppam. Here, Mandeen and her various teams, each working on a different project, cluster together on plastic chairs and discuss progress. She is fluent in each project, and explains the science of coastal reclamation like it's obvious; unfortunately, when she is finished, coastal erosion does seem scarily inevitable.

Ports and harbours require breakwaters—manmade structures that jut out from the coast—which interfere with the natural drifting of sand up and down a beach. This in turn causes extreme erosion of the sandy beach, allowing the water to encroach upon settlements and eat into navigable coastline. After building a port and breakwater in 1986 that protruded about 250 meters, the designers of the port installed a sand bypass system to artificially move the sand between the two stretches of beach that were now divided by the structure. But this system was hardly put to use by the Pondicherry government, resulting in severe erosion of the beach going northwards to almost 7 kilometres from the port. Beaches which had been over 100 metres wide were completely gone.

What was once 4 kilometres of accessible beach and Promenade running parallel to Pondicherry has shrunk to 1.5 kilometres of waves hitting tetrapods, and villages north and south of this are suffering. Any interventions so far have only exacerbated the problem. For example, creating stone barriers to concentrate sand in one area means erosion elsewhere; the stones unavoidably sink, requiring more stones, which becomes increasingly expensive without being a permanent solution.

132

In 2007 a ₹2,500-crore container port was being planned. Mandeen calls this a 'land scam' and the measures taken since then even more rapacious. 'Were these informed decisions? One thousand percent *not*!'

She rifles through a 223-page policy report prepared by PondyCAN, along with Bombay Natural History Society (BNHS) and Tata Institute of Social Sciences (TISS), titled *The Challenged Coast of India*. If India moves ahead with its plan to construct 300-odd ports and harbours along the subcontinent's coast, the country is doomed. Current regulations are 'non-transparent, unaccountable, and unscientific', warns leading environmentalist Sunita Narain in the Foreword, before Mandeen and her colleagues present various recommendations in the subsequent 200 pages. For visual learners, wildlife and conservation filmmaker Shekar Dattatri has prepared a fifteen-minute documentary called *India's Disappearing Beaches: A Wake Up Call* which PondyCAN has screened all over Pondicherry, as well as in Chennai and Delhi.

Akash Kapur, a writer who has grown up around these beaches, wrote an essay for *Granta* in 2008 deploring their shrinkages and its toll on surrounding fisher communities, such as the village of Chinnamudaliarchavadi, just north of Pondicherry. In Kapur's words, 'At least thirty metres of beach have been lost in just a few months. The narrow band of sand that remains drops quickly into the ocean, like a cliff, a sign of rapid erosion. Men and women walk up and down what is left of the beach, a vacant, perhaps incredulous, look in their eyes. The sea is crowded with empty boats. They used to lie on the sand, but now the fishermen have to row out to their craft in flimsy catamarans.'

Sebastien Cortés's photo essay *Pondicherry*, published by Roli Books, shows the beach diminishing from one page to the next. The book came out in 2012 but his pictures feature a Pondicherry several years older than that, as seen in the calendars from the early 2000s that are caught in his frames. His shots show a much more spacious beach than today's version: unlike his photographs, there are no longer wooden shacks for sunset meditations, or room for crowds to gather and immerse idols during the annual Ganesh Chaturthi or

Masimagam festivals. The first of three essays in his book allude drily to the eroding beach as a '[p]aradoxe intéressant'. French writer Pascal Bruckner claims that 'this narrow strip of land has turned its back on the ocean'. For reasons he does not elaborate upon, but which Mandeen and her team have made quite clear, the currents are 'dangereux', and as the erosion increases, any scope for a fishing industry has been rendered 'archaïque'.

Photographs and interviews recall that in the 1960s, the beach used to be a stretch of sandy coast from the Ashram playground up to the Gandhi statue. Behind the statue, the pier stuck out 'like a finger' into the sea, and received the smaller boats ferrying cargo from the larger ships anchored farther out. The southern side of the pier was for the boats, and not accessible for recreation. Mandeen explains that when this pier fell apart in the sixties, a new pier was built further south, and here too ships would anchor out at sea and have their cargo brought in by tugboats. It was operational until the port was built even further south at the mouth of the Ariyankuppam estuary, not far from Arikamedu. Just beyond the new piers were fishing hamlets and beautiful beaches, all of which disappeared after the port was built.

Fifty years later, the landscape is completely different: the Old Port building is now a café; it had collapsed due to erosion and was restored after the rock seawall was installed to protect the Promenade.

The 'beach', which is really a walking path, stretches out on both sides. The new pier pokes into the water half a kilometre farther south, an even longer finger—so, visually, the middle one.

Port-related work, from talks to planning, development, construction, judicial interventions, environmental clearances, and more, has been ongoing in Pondicherry since the 1970s. The latest legal story reflects how ardently environmental groups have pitted themselves against any kind of port development. After Pondicherry's government approved the building of a new port in 2006, environmental group Villianur Iyarkai Padukappu Maiyam (Villianur Nature Conservation Centre) filed a case in the Madras High Court to reverse the decision. When the high court dismissed the group's request, the group appealed to the Supreme Court, whose 126-page ruling in 2009 was in favour of construction. Undaunted, Pondicherry's environmentalists applied pressure in various government offices, until the union Ministry of Home Affairs intervened in 2013 and, for reasons unrelated to the judicial process, ordered the government to cancel their contract with the consortium of developers who had been sanctioned to build the port seven years earlier. The private contractors are now taking legal action because of what they deem to be an illegal termination of their contract, but Mandeen says this case was dropped too, with no liability to the government.

'The port continues to loom over Pondy,' she warns.

There is now an agreement between the Pondicherry government and the Madras port to bring cargo here by barges. 'Cruise shipping is mentioned too!' But regular dredging will have to be done so that the beaches are nourished and restored, none of which is planned for.

Mandeen writes: 'The PondyCAN team has been pursuing the restoration of the beach which has disappeared due to the man-made erosion, all 7 kilometres of it, some of it in Tamil Nadu, since its inception in 2007. The Ministry of Earth Sciences decided to fund the northern nearshore reef which is part of the total Pondicherry Beach restoration project. Its design is quite state of the art and unique, and the whole world is watching to see its inaugural implementation. Once completed it is expected to hold the sand in front of the town, to fill the hole caused by the erosion, realign the coast which went totally out of alignment due to the erosion, and allow sand to flow over this underwater reef. That way, once the hole in front of the town is filled, and beaches start appearing, the beaches northward will be nourished by the flowing sand and all the lost beaches will be restored. But for this to happen, it is important that the sand is not allowed to go on accumulating south of the port but flow northwards. Activating the original sand bypassing would be required as well as a redesign of the current harbour to suit current requirements and minimize the sand bypassing costs.'

PondyCAN has been working since March 2017 to

restore part of the beach, and has successfully recreated a small patch in front of the Secretariat. Mandeen sends a series of photos via WhatsApp: families, children, and couples enjoying the waves. 'Once a good stretch of beach appears along the whole beach Promenade, this will encourage other places in the country to take up beach restoration—this is already happening, but only marginally so.'

Judgements and newspaper articles alike mention that the 'history of the Pondicherry Port dates back to the tenth century A.D.'—another reminder that the city is far older than its tourism, its boutiques and its scuba diving. And that preservation of this ancient land and coast is a necessary responsibility. So far the city's strong civic sense, the people's love for their beaches, and Sri Aurobindo Ashram's nature-conscious behaviour, have proved to be a combination strong enough to reckon with the highest echelons of government.

÷

PondyCAN's documentary was screened midway through Pondicherry's month-long Heritage Festival in 2018, followed by a 'field visit along the coast'. Other festival events included community yoga; walking tours; craft bazaars; photography contests; Quranic recitation; museum exhibits and traditional theatre. Now in its fourth year, the Pondicherry Heritage Festival has become an annual celebration of the city's cultural, historic, environmental, and artistic activities. It is organized by

INTACH, PondyCAN and People for Pondy Heritage, and boasts a long list of partners, from private hotels to the Pondicherry Department of Tourism. During the 2018 festival, children were received in the French Consulate garden and given colouring books containing pictures of heritage sites in the union territory, from Arikamedu to Aayi Mandapam. Other venues hosted live performances such as the previously encountered Odissi dancer Aneesh Raghavan, and screened movies like Ang Lee's *Life of Pi*, whose protagonist is from Pondicherry. A new event featured Indochina, or modern-day Vietnam, which was a contemporaneous French colony. There was a Vietnamese food festival and open houses of Vietnamese families long settled in Pondicherry. Outdoors at Ossudu Lake, ornithologist Bubesh Gupta and birders enjoyed sighting myriad different species around the water body.

'Once our minds are focused and our priorities are clear,' reads the festival's mission statement, 'we must act with passion and purpose to preserve those things that make Pondicherry unique within India and, indeed, place it among the most interesting cities of the world.' Big words for a small place, but the festival sponsors and organizers believe strongly in Pondicherry's potential to be something much larger than its dot-sized presence on the map. Ashok Panda, Co-Convener of INTACH Pondicherry, and with the team for over fifteen years, is constantly looking at different projects, from building restoration to cultural heritage, from improved transportation to more accurate street signs that reflect today's population and its languages. His long nose accentuates his lean frame; he is often seen around town leading yet another walking tour.

The INTACH office, an elegantly restored Tamil home with a sun-drenched courtyard in the middle, is wall-papered with posters showing structures before and after restoration work: streets before and after major clean-ups; the Promenade before and after its recent makeover. Photo albums and oversized books are piled on tables for visitors to browse through and inspect various INTACH projects in greater detail. One flight up are more rooms where project teams sit around cluttered tables to discuss upcoming activities. One team is especially proud of the furniture in their room; what appears to be a long, thick, wooden tabletop is actually a very old doorway that has been given legs and converted into a sturdy and stylish surface.

INTACH began its work in Pondicherry in 1985, focusing on architectural conservation, restoration, urban landscaping, street management, and other civic projects. Although completely self-funded, the group works very closely with the Pondicherry government, which has allowed INTACH to have a large presence and impact in the city. 'Whenever there's a government meeting, the word "heritage" just has to pop up, and the Culture Ministry will say, "Where's INTACH; why isn't INTACH involved with this?"' says Shubham Biswas, who spent nearly two years in Pondicherry

139

and whose projects focused on the city's 'intangible cultural heritage'. In addition to renovating and restoring buildings, INTACH works to make these spaces economically viable, not just through tourism, but for the locals as well. 'When you're doing a restoration, the easiest part is to get the buildings and the streets in order, but what follows is the people utilizing these spaces. Have you brought *them* up to date with the buildings and what they're used for?' Biswas asks. 'We want to make these buildings and their surroundings economically viable, and we use cultural heritage awareness—documentation, video clips and brochures—to make the public who live here more involved in this process.'

From the redevelopment of the Promenade to upgraded street signs, from the smartly renovated Tamil homes to the colonnaded French houses-turned-boutique hotels, Pondicherry's cultural heritage is garnering more interest from locals and outsiders. In 2017, Pondicherry was selected by the central government as one of 100 cities to be developed into 'Smart Cities', whose definition encompasses a number of civic plans from inclusive housing to accessible open and green spaces, to being more walkable, to being more resource-efficient.

Panda is earnest about building a transportation system that is economic and eco-friendly. He has been looking for a solution to the city's vehicular congestion for nearly two decades, and his electric vehicle pilot in 2004 is proof. Fifteen years ago, INTACH and the

Pondicherry government introduced these vehicles onto the streets and went as far as installing battery stations around the city, all as part of 'Asia Urbs', a collaboration with European agencies to 'achieve urban economic and environmental goals through heritage preservation initiatives'. 'The idea was to replace diesel and petrol vehicles with electric, as has happened in Agra and other heritage precincts...' Biswas says. Although the electric vehicles were only a test run, other projects have been much more permanent, such as making the beach boulevard car-free every evening. A new project is underway now to turn the streets parallel to the beach—rues Dumas, Suffren, and Romain Rolland— car-free on different days of the week.

The Smart Cities Mission addresses three needs for any urban space: city improvement or retrofitting; city renewal or redevelopment; and city extension or greenfield development. Pondicherry applied twice with some focus on the greenfield category and was rejected both times; they were accepted on their third attempt as a candidate for city renewal, to focus on the city's cultural heritage. Now, several organizations are working together to finalize Pondicherry's proposal: the Public Works Department, Tourism Department and Culture Ministry Department, Agence Française de Développement in France, and INTACH in a consulting role.

Locals and officials are excited for more solar panelling, fewer motorcycles on the streets, and traditional architecture made accessible. And while the Smart Cities project has brought singular attention to these causes, the Heritage Festival is a yearly reminder that Pondicherry's ecological, civic and cultural aptitude is only growing. Mandeen recalls a festival event from a few years ago, organized by Justice Annoussamy, whom she calls 'an eminent Pondicherrian'. People assembled in his home, a beautiful Tamil house with a sprawling garden in the back, to discuss a range of topics about their city. Mandeen summarizes what was brought up: 'What's special about Pondicherry; what keeps us here; what brings us back?'

The nonagenarian Annoussamy is as prolific about his hometown as he is reticent about his own life. Perhaps a professional habit, Justice Annoussamy prefers to pass judgement on his city without revealing any personal opinions. This makes conversation tricky, but not impossible. Bespectacled and bald but for a strip of grey hair around the back of his head, he moves slowly and speaks deliberately, and prefers that the conversation take place in French.

'Read my book,' he says in a growling bass, in answer to my preliminary questions about the city's history and geography, referring to *L'Intermède français en Inde: Secousses politiques et mutations juridiques*, written by him and published by the French Institute in 2005. The bass intensifies when he is asked more subjective questions about Pondicherry. Why are so many people drawn to it?

He counters with his own questions: What draws anyone to any city? What appealed to you about New York? My answer—that New York City is a place where you can discover yourself—he volleys right back: You will find this in Chicago, Tokyo, Peking, London. The differences between them are negligible. 'Les Pondicheriens n'ont aucune idée de Pondichéry'; the people don't have an idea of Pondicherry. When pressed on this, he clarifies that Pondy lives in 'l'imagination de gens', the people's imagination, as does any city. Trying to capture it in words can never measure up to how a person feels about their home or the stories they inherit in swearing allegiance to a place. The implicit meaning seems to be that probing an elderly man for quotable quotes about his city will be futile, and so the interview ends with a promise to look up his book at the Institute, and parting words of admiration for his polylingual book collection. Spines of Lorca stand at attention in the foyer, which provoke a last attempt from me to understand the Chief Justice, this time through his taste for romantic and spiritual poetry. But the answer is yet another grunt, revealing nothing about his literary preferences. 'The Lorca belongs to my wife.'

NINE

Also Known As

There is a local pot dealer in Pondicherry who changes his name every few months to avoid being caught. For a spell, he was Shadowdust. Sometime later, Ki. When people call the number he's given them, they ask anna for an auto, because Shadowdust, or Ki, also drives an autorickshaw, which is convenient when fixing a location for the handoff. Once the customer has spotted Shadowdust in his auto, both approach the other slowly, by foot, and wait for Shadowdust to turn into a nearby alley where the transaction can take place. In a discreet exchange of greetings, money and goods have swapped hands. The whole thing has taken under thirty seconds, which is too fast for me to keep track of what is happening. I try to introduce myself, hand extended, but contact—and contact details—are limited in such situations, and my inexperience makes the other parties smile.

But the interaction is worth it. Just a day later, at a busy coffee stand within the boulevards, I see Shadowdust or Ki or the auto kaaran in a new avatar, this time chatty and eager. Recognizing me, he introduces himself as a tour guide, currently assisting an Australian tourist who is visiting from the Ramana Maharshi Ashram, two and a half hours away. He can recommend hotels and give guided tours in English, if anyone is interested, and I am tempted by this change in personality. In a city this small, recognition is an asymptotic graph that tends towards the inevitable, so Shadowdust or Ki the auto kaaran-cum-tour-guide has to be careful. One only hopes that his latest nom de guerre is as creative as earlier variants.

It is common for Pondicherrians, also known as Pondichériens or Pondichériennes—to be doubles and triples of themselves. Whether in name, language, geographic residence, profession, religion, or some other category, the populace is inherently mixed. Or mixed up. 'Like an idiyappam,' Yuvaraj says over dinner one rainy evening, referring to the dish he is eating.

÷

Just a few streets away in the Hindu Quarter is a colourful two-storey building sandwiched between Tamil-style houses and three kovils. The sign hanging on the front door reads 'La Casita'. The staircase from the street leads visitors to a large open space with wooden flooring, wall-to-wall mirrors and shelves holding yoga mats, books, and souvenirs from all around the world. Posters advertise dance and fitness workshops for Pondicherrians of all ages, backgrounds and levels.

An even narrower staircase, each step painted a

different colour, leads to the terrace also known as the Traveller's Café. At the end of this vertical rainbow is an equally cheerful space with low-lying tables and stools. Sunlight pools on the floor under the thatched roof, and behind it, temple gopurams taper into the sky. Menus offer a variety of hot drinks and snacks including Tibetan momos and Nepali aloo. La Casita's website notes that 'WiFi available BUT to initiate the concept of socializing in real world, WiFi is chargeable.'

Enter Kelsang Doma, or Kash for short. Her name is Tibetan, she grew up in Delhi, and now lives in Pondicherry, teaching people to salsa. Looking back, she says, her favourite part of her Delhi life was learning from her Venezuelan teacher, who 'showed us the essence' of dance. Kash started teaching, too, but wasn't enjoying the experience. She found Pondicherry during her travels around the country. 'I thought, eureka!' She decided to shift her business down south.

The North Indian transplant started La Casita in March 2014 to bring Latin American culture and dance to Pondicherry. She is petite, with Tibetan features, a from-all-over Indian accent, and a permanent smile on her face. Her studio offers lessons in Cuban and Afro-Cuban dance.

The reactions have been mixed. In such a small city, word spreads quickly and Kash's Zumba classes have filled up—'the women come wearing saris, and they are amazing'. But in a neighbourhood and a culture dominated by traditional, conservative Tamil values,

Latin American dance can appear too sensual. 'Salsa has grown, but my tango class is empty.' So Kash is persistent, and her monthly salsa socials are becoming more popular. On 1 April 2016, 'International Rueda de Casino Flash Mob Day', La Casita organized its first flash mob on the Promenade. Girls with mallipoo in their hair and boys in kurtas, many wearing tilaks, expertly twirled partners and stepped right-left-right, left-right-left. 'I love the contrast; they have become the best dancers,' Kash gushes. A year later, they held their second annual flash mob, this time in matching outfits and looking more professional.

The late morning heat chases passers-by indoors and upstairs, where they scatter across the tables. Some are regulars at La Casita, others are tourists who have found the studio in *Lonely Planet* and come for the 'cosy rooftop travellers' café'. Two men are in serious discussion about vipassana meditation, and phrases like 'unseen forces' and 'energy and sub-energies' rise into the air. Another table's conversation takes place in Spanish. Many know each other; Kash recognizes all of them. This was always her goal, and something she could not achieve in Delhi. 'You needed to be in the circle,' she says, about the network-obsessed capital. In Pondicherry, it is the opposite: everyone seems to know everyone. 'Here there are many circles for such a small space. But it's easier to connect,' which is what Kash needs to promote La Casita and its dance culture beyond the boulevards. Perched lightly on a stool, she requests two coffees from her staff. 'I became more relaxed after coming here,' she says. She has plans to add a quiet reading space in her café where dancers, travellers and locals can seek stillness in between all the movement.

The farther one moves from White Town, the harder it is for Kash to communicate her vision. Finding new venues for her socials is a painstaking process since she has to explain the concept each time. '"What's a dance party?" they all ask me.' Some venues request that men and women not mingle. Others demand hefty covers. This scepticism is not unexpected in small-town South India, but in Pondicherry, the idea of choreographed partner dances is slowly catching on. Kash can identify only one place, Café L'-E-Space, that played salsa music, where customers would get up and dance 'without any issues' with the management. Now there is a second— the restaurant-bar-boutique DisDis & Co, where Kash's 'Afro-Latin' parties bring in at least a hundred people each month. The music is carefully selected to encourage dancers of all levels to approach the floor. Some men are eager to escort a partner into the crowd, but dance etiquette requires that they only approach women who are standing and not sitting, and ask for one song at a time. The visual of local men and women moving their bodies in ways utterly unlike a Tamil movie sequence triggers some cognitive dissonance, but for me it's a chance to indulge in some good flânerie. Especially when some dancers, their tongues loosened by drink, are happy to share their stories.

In between turns and twists, using Tamil and English, a stocky man named Mani tells his. He grew up in a village near Auroville, where his farmer parents sacrificed everything to fund their oldest son's education. But he failed the tenth grade, 'fell in love with dancing', and learned to salsa for free from a German teacher living nearby. His brother has a postgraduate degree in bio-engineering and his sister is in her fourth year of higher studies, but Mani has no professional prospects. He just loves to dance. 'Add me on Facebook,' he requests breathlessly, before moving on to find another partner.

The evening at DisDis is interrupted when the staff wheel out a birthday cake on a tray. The crowd gathers around and promptly sings 'Happy Birthday' to an elderly Tamil woman dressed in a special-occasion sari and beaming at the scene. Cake is cut and distributed— typical of any staid family celebration, except this backdrop happens to be a swanky restaurant and bar. People use the time to begin or continue conversations with others at the social. The birthday woman's son, Arun, calls himself 'the real slumdog millionaire' from the 'urban slum' of Pondicherry, who received his master's degree in Psychology from a university in Germany, near Berlin. His schedule is too busy for an interview to talk more about his 'cultural psychologist' practice in Pondicherry. 'Google me!' he suggests.

After several birthday photos, the woman and her

entourage return to their table, and the music resumes. One dancer has brought her young daughter with her, whose enthusiasm on the floor elicits claps and cheers. Kash moves through the crowd, hugging people in greeting and in gratitude. Her husband, Romain Timmers, a head-shorn lanky Frenchman, is close behind, and immediately conspicuous for his above-average height and versatile moves on the dance floor.

Back at the Traveller's Café, Kash describes him as a 'modern circus artist' whose focus is juggling, balancing, and vertical dance. They met in Pondicherry, which, I'm convinced, is exactly where a dancer and a juggler should meet. Thanks to Timmers, La Casita offers acrobatics and acro-yoga workshops in addition to its Bollywood, salsa, and fitness classes.

But the studio isn't only interested in pushing boundaries. One of the Zumba Fitness classes is 'LADIES ONLY', and the yoga classes are conducted in 'Tamil (mostly)', reminding everyone that La Casita's monthly parties and visiting capoeira teachers are still aspirational for many Pondicherrians. What the majority are seeking is perhaps more conventional, but definitely universal: fun ways to lose weight and opportunities to meet people. An hour in La Casita's rooftop café proves that these things happen on a regular basis.

÷

Kash's hope to introduce new forms of movement, dance, and living into Pondicherry has echoes less than 15 kilometres north in Auroville. Often mixed up, the two are distinct entities geographically, culturally and philosophically, but are constantly taking their cues from each other. That Auroville has already been mentioned a handful of times in a biography about a completely different place says a lot about their relationship. Akash Kapur, an Aurovilian since childhood and an internationally published author, describes the community as a 'living laboratory: a not-quite-yet defined experiment, an incipient society searching for new models of economy, politics, aesthetics, culture'.

To commemorate the fiftieth anniversary of Auroville in 2018, Kapur compiled an anthology of prose and poetry written by 'Aurovilians' about their city, their utopia, their home. The 300 pages rarely repeat descriptions or ideas, which says something about how vibrantly the community was envisioned, and the richness that residents continue to draw from it. The 'City of Dawn' takes its name from 'aurore', or dawn in French, and not, as is generally assumed, from Sri Aurobindo.

151

The Mother had the idea to build Auroville in the 1960s. It was formally inaugurated on 28 February 1968, by which point she was ninety years old. In her essay in the anthology, educator and sustainability consultant Bindu Mohanty describes how 'representatives of 124 nations and 23 Indian states placed a handful of earth in a lotus-shaped urn, thereby symbolically founding Auroville as a city of human unity'.

City of Dawn. City of human unity. Names and synonyms abound for a place where people from all over the globe congregate and live in a peace made tangible by sincere idealism, environmental sensitivity, and sheer joy. Over 2,500 people from about fifty countries uprooted themselves from established homes and societies and moved to 'an inhospitable desert' spread over 20 kilometres of rural area interspersed with village and private lands, where they forged friendships with their rural Tamil neighbours while planting over 20 lakh trees. But the afforestation prompted deeper thoughts about living off the earth. 'Aren't we here to try and create a model society...where the horizon is wide, the taste of life is sweet and its beauty immeasurable?' asks an Aurovilian in his essay. It stands to reason that a city of human unity should be a model society—a 'city the earth needs', insists another Aurovilian. 'We are here to grow in consciousness, not build a city.'

Originally inspired by Sri Aurobindo's Integral Yoga and then shaped by the Mother, the city—or consciousness—of Auroville is a mixed up place, inherently multi-everything. Culture, language, resources, capabilities and infrastructure are just a few variables here, perhaps causing Kapur to describe the community as 'elusive, elliptical, tenaciously inconsistent', but whose syncopations inevitably march towards harmony and resonance. Another resident defines life in Auroville as a 'vastly complex process in which diverse individuals with very different perspectives, collide, embrace, fracture and cross-fertilize as a "softening up", a preparation, for some kind of change of transformation'.

Call it a 'City of the Future' then, in which all individual differences are subsumed by the values of the community, such as a shared economy; money is to be 'a medium of exchange only with the outside world'. 'A City of Yoga', another essay offers, where all residents 'work five hours daily for the common good'. Or even a 'City of Immortality' that 'belongs to humanity as a whole'; the Indian Parliament conferred the legal status of a foundation onto Auroville in 1988.

Thirty years later, its assets continue to grow through 'personal resources, donations and grants [which] are collectively held by the community and accountable to the Auroville Foundation'. But the concept of an elevated awareness and an energized empathy is as strong for the city-foundation's long-term residents as it was when dawn first rose over its then-barren plains. A French poet and publisher chronicles Auroville meetings where 'it is easy to decry the threads rising from each and every head and converging towards the mighty hand of some weaver above'. Kapur expresses a similar sentiment: 'I always had a sense of being surrounded by natural poets; there is an inherent lyricism to life in Auroville that should be fertile ground for literature.'

No wonder so many encounters with Aurovilians have left me scrambling for a pen to write down what was just said. A total stranger was all smiles when speaking a few words to me from his hospital bed; another invited me to dinner in the depths of Auroville to meet a local troupe that trains in the ancient South Indian martial art of kalaripayattu; a third shared her Tamil poetry at a vocational school she runs; the fourth was Kapur himself.

And yet, the 'City with a Soul' is only at 5 per cent of its predicted population of 50,000 residents, and the Mother's imagination that relationships normally based 'on competition and strife' would be replaced by relationships of 'collaboration and real brotherhood', is very much a work in progress. Mohanty details Auroville's 5,000-strong hired labour force which comes primarily from the surrounding villages, and tourism that attracts more than 90,000 visitors per year; these influxes 'bring about developments that are not always in keeping with the community's ideals'.

Utopia isn't easy. But Auroville is still at it, fifty years later. Call it a laboratory, an experiment, a 'city of' whatever impulse or emotion brought someone here—but acknowledge it as something real, living, and growing. One of the essay titles sums it up best: a 'Paradox Town'.

÷

A Californian in his sixties, Curtis John Degler has been lucky with the 'Planetary City', also known as Auroville, where he works as a scuba diving instructor, the 'first professional certificate-offering scuba instructor in the entire eastern part of mainland India', adding that no one has refuted this claim yet. He divides his time between Auroville and Mahabalipuram—also known as Mamallapuram—a town in Tamil Nadu about ninety minutes north of Pondicherry, and the site of several seventh- and eighth-century historic rock temples from the Pallava dynasty. Living just a few minutes from these ancient temples and carvings, Degler is preoccupied with another age-old tradition: caste. Specifically, the Irula community, who are spread out over several one-street villages on the outskirts of Mamallapuram. They are a snake-catcher tribe, 'the lowest of the low; the Dalits of the Dalits,' he says.

This limits the men's ability to earn regularly and consistently, even though they also find work as coolie-labourers engaged in wood cutting. So Degler has turned his focus to the Irula women, for whom he has built, and funds, a non-profit that sells their handmade crafts. He founded the Kanimar Artisanal Hand Embroidery Project, which has now become a physical shop in Mamallapuram, and is the source of economic independence for many of the Irula women.

Degler is relentless, constantly talking about the Irula families he knows, issuing them microloans, providing flood relief after unprecedented, heavy rains in 2015, and helping educate their children. 'I'm terrible at marketing,' he confesses, so he just relies on the snakes to impress his audiences. Recounting yet another incident when an Irula man showed Degler a cobra he had recently caught, the American described the man emerging from his one-room home holding a pillowcase. 'What was the difference between a regular pillow cover and the one in his hand?' he asked me.

And then, without waiting for an answer, he responded, 'The one in his hand *hissed*.'

Tales such as these invariably attract intrepid travellers and animal lovers to his small operation in Mamallapuram, where, in addition to meeting the women or visiting a school, they can also go on a snake-hunt with some of the Irula men. Degler regularly offers his guests the single room on the terrace two floors above his apartment. Stepping onto the rooftop, a dusty paperback in hand, I enjoy a sunset-glazed view of a Tamil town whose past is more alive than its present.

Living in Mamallapuram is not the same as living in Pondicherry: tourists can manage with English, but long-term residents need Tamil. Degler's is passable; his connection to Tamil began when he studied the language at the University of Chicago. The more he loved the language, the more he hated 'university spaces'. Reading books like *Notes on Love in a Tamil Family*, a detailed ethnography written by anthropologist Margaret Trawick—his classmate back in Chicago—he felt drawn to the dynamics and narratives of that part of the world. So, after retiring, he packed a few possessions and arrived in South India in 2003.

From there, Degler's story synchronizes with that of

many foreigners settled in Auroville and Pondicherry: a sudden love for the place; a long-overdue escape from somewhere else; an instinctive empathy for the locals. A passionate diver, Degler also had a new marine and coastal landscape to explore. With his Tamil proficiency and laidback Californian attitude, he easily made friends. It is no surprise that the Irulas found him— or the other way around. Today they are each other's biggest support.

÷

Of course there are plenty of expats who run heritage hotels within the boulevards, many of whom dress and eat like locals, and commute from their home to their office on bicycles, looking like Indian schoolchildren— or grown up Parisians. Scholars and academics are a common sight on the Promenade, making their way between the various archives. Tourists from all over India, and of the international backpacking variety, are excited by the beaches, the scuba diving, the rooftop cafés and the croissants. And so, Pondicherry is India's pamphlet-friendly advertisement for post-colonial European heritage.

But these idiyappam Pondicherrians and Aurovilians are special. Like Shadowdust, their identities are changing, too: from foreigner to local; stranger to neighbour; juggler to dancer; from Auroville member to Pondicherry citizen; from student to practitioner; from dance classes to pop-up performances. They reflect something much deeper about Pondicherry's multiple identities: that this is a city too small for strangers to stay unknown, too coastal for concrete to overwhelm nature, too Européenne to become fully Tamil. One wonders what an ethnography about Pondicherry might yield. Happily, one can turn to the city's many libraries to find out.

TEN

Bibliothèques et Bibliophiles

As of 2017, *the city within the boulevards has six* libraries, and several smaller archives. Extend the area to include Pondicherry University, and the number increases by one state-of-the-art, fully digitized library. For a city whose hub of activity, trade and information is so compact, this is an impressive, even bizarre number. In university towns abroad, the high ratio of bookshops and libraries can be explained by the academic institution that looms large enough to provide business to cafés, bars and movie theatres. But Pondicherry is not a conventional university town. Rather, its scholarly funding and collections come from sources that transcend any single institution. Central government money runs the 800-acre Pondicherry University while the French government maintains its legacy in the French Institute of Pondicherry, L'École Française d'Extrême-Orient (L'EFEO) and L'Alliance Française. Sri Aurobindo Ashram runs the Ashram Library, Ashram Archives, and Ashram Press. The local government manages the city's Romain Rolland Library, the Pondicherry Museum, and the dusty, one-room Puducherry Archives.

And then there are the smaller collections tucked into the Subramania Bharathi Museum; INTACH office; Mission Church Press; Pondicherry's Historical Society; and the environmentalist office of PondyCAN.

Walking distance from all of these (except the university library) are five bookstores. The most visited is Focus Bookshop which shows off one table of Pondicherry-themed books, mostly of the coffee-table variety. *Pondicherry*, featuring photography by Sebastien Cortés, catches my eye. The back cover is a landscape view of the ever-photogenic Promenade at dusk: pairs of men walking in one direction; a trio of women in the other; couples in mid-conversation; and a bright blue food cart in the centre of the frame, the two food-sellers' backs to the viewer. A seductive blurb describes Pondicherry in English and in French: 'An Eden that is hard to fathom and does not unveil itself at once, it opens its heart of secrets only to the deserving.' Across the aisle, P. Raja's books take up half a shelf, starting with *Glimpses of Pondicherry*, a brief historical narrative about the city, and moving into thicker history books.

Higginbothams is an older bookshop, remembered by previous generations. Located just off Nehru Street it is more visible to tourists and shoppers. Its offerings are generic, current—and perhaps most usefully, include student study guides in a number of subjects. Librarie Kailash (librarie in French means bookshop, not library) stocks books printed by Edition Kailash: these specialize in 'franco-indienne' narratives including 'voyageurs d'hier et d'aujourd'hui'—adventurers of yesterday and today; and 'romanciers français et asiatiques'—French and Asian novelists (the French word for novel is un roman, hence its author is un romancier). There is the Ashram bookstore—two, actually—SABDA and VAK, that sell Ashram publications and related spiritual books. But reserve room for the second-hand bookstores on Mission Street and Rue Suffren whose signs loudly announce gigantic sales and near-free books. In these dimly lit high-ceilinged shops stocked with flimsy children's books, paperback bestsellers and comic versions of various historical narratives, employees are usually in their own quiet haze of boredom. Wait for the occasional high-pitched argument in rapid-fire Tamil, as sometimes happens; it may spark a customer—as it did me—into buying something completely unnecessary.

161

Pondicherry's literary persona is not complete without mentioning the private libraries of certain citizens. P. Raja's collection of over 60,000 books occupies an entire floor of his house, in shelves that line the walls and touch both floor and ceiling. Justice Annoussamy is a similarly ardent bibliophile whose house layout allows the bookshelves to form its perimeter. And when Victor Paulin, a retired soldat, received me in his home for an impromptu interview in January 2017, he spent as much time sharing stories as he did barking at his servant to locate a particular book in the piles stacked all around his massive living room—a room that was featured, Madame Paulin added proudly, in a photobook of Pondicherry heritage homes—which was published by Pondicherry's own Lycée Français in 1996.

To recap: six libraries, five bookstores, four museums. In an area roughly 1.5 km x 1.5 km.

÷

One of the first markers of Pondicherry for anyone travelling into the city on ECR from Chennai are the wide gates of Pondicherry University, inside which lies a sprawling, sylvan campus. But if one enters the gates in an autorickshaw or on a two-wheeler and heads to the library several turns away, one is rewarded with a sight entirely unlike the 'bohemian-chic, New Age-meets-Old World hang-out' image Pondicherry has in *Lonely Planet*.

What the guidebook has not accounted for is the university's Head Librarian, R. Samyuktha, a feisty, smiling woman who pounces on government grants, liberally quotes her mentors and favourite authors, and believes in a digital future for research. She repeats her maxim that a library must have an 'irresistible ambience'. No matter a student's age, background, subject interest or need for a book, once they enter her library, they should never want to leave.

Samyuktha has done everything to transform the university resource into a timeless archive. Under her leadership, Pondicherry University's library became the third in the country to adopt the RFID system for all of its collections. It was one of three 'test beds' in 2012 for a digital search software, and the second university library in India to digitize and upload all of its student theses into a national digital repository. Samyuktha is helping grow a government initiative called ENLIST, which is building a national library infrastructure for students throughout India to access 'crores worth of material' at their fingertips.

Walking around the library—80,000 square feet between two buildings—through the different student reading halls, digital collections, reference rooms, and auditoriums, Samyuktha points to a million small details she's incorporated into her architectural design. The auditorium has a ramped entrance for wheelchair-bound students. Plug points are placed at eye level in the student cubicles, instead of impossible-to-reach corners. The chair and sofa upholstery are in soothing colours, windows are large and overlook tree-lined sidewalks, whose greenery she has also nurtured. Air-conditioner wires have been tucked into bathrooms and storage cupboards so that the walls they are installed on are clutter-free. Large walls are painted bright yellow and some of the blank ones are to be filled with collages of student photography. Bookshelves in the reference section, bursting with fat encyclopaedias, have been reinforced with additional brackets so that they do not sag in the centre. 'The designers liked my idea so much,' she says with a grin, 'they've used it in other libraries!'

Like any good librarian, Samyuktha is thorough

163

with her sources and citations. Pondicherry University is only thirty years old and, while its digital collections and student archives are thriving, it does not carry rare documents. That kind of material can be found in the French Institute; in Auroville; or farther away in the University of Madras—itself a heritage university. But this is not a problem for Samyuktha. 'Pondicherry can give you leads to content,' she promises. 'It's like a referral service.'

Indeed, continuing south on the main road from the university gates will lead any scholar into Pondicherry Town, where several other research venues await. The aforementioned French Institute, along with L'EFEO, possesses unrivalled collections in Sanskritology, Indology, Tamil History and Literature. According to L'EFEO librarian Shanty Rayapoullé, the two started as one organization in 1954, but evolved over time into two different repositories of French history in India, ultimately splitting in 2003. L'EFEO receives its funding from France's Ministry of Education and Research, while the French Institute is funded by the Ministry of Foreign Affairs. Both libraries are housed in elegant French buildings; even though the L'EFEO structure was undergoing heavy renovation in 2017, its scrap-filled courtyards, tall window shutters clapping in the sea breeze, and artwork on the paint-peeling walls revealed proud European potential. Leaving one's shoes at the base of the staircase on the ground floor of the L'EFEO building guarantees that one will return to dust-covered shoes a few hours later, but the various collections breathe comfortably one and two floors above the construction work, peering out through glass-cased shelves that are wiped clean daily.

Rayapoullé is fluent in the institution's history and current purpose, having started work there as a secretary nearly fifteen years ago. Freshly back from France where she grew up, and trying to reclaim Pondicherry as her home, Rayapoullé took time to adjust to the place, the people, and the work. In spite of her typical Tamil features—complexion, attire, long hair in a braid—she feels different. 'I'm finding myself as a stranger here,' she notes mild-manneredly, seated at a desk covered with books in three languages. 'They make me feel it,' she adds, meaning the Pondicherry locals who, I have observed, use various techniques—some intrusive; others not—to ascertain a stranger's identity. In a town this small, where all the librarians know each other; where all the expats meet for cigarettes and coffee in the same WiFi-enabled cafés, and for drinks and flirting at Santhi Inn on Thursday nights; where everyone knows when Kash's next pop-up salsa party will be—in this town, looking Indian but holding a French passport; being fair-skinned but speaking fluent Tamil; using French funding to further Sanskrit scholarship; being interested in Pondicherry but not Auroville—all of these choices affect a person's Pondicherry-ness. As a foreign-educated rusty-Tamil-speaker making little claim to the city except as a second-generation descendant,

I have evaded this kind of judgement. But where does Rayapoullé fit into the city's matrix, which is far more labyrinthine than its gridded layout and its alphabetized book shelves? She laughs and points at her nameplate on the door to her office. 'I'm nothing more than a chicken!' she laughs, playing on the French word poulet, which sounds exactly like the second half of her last name.

The soft-spoken librarian has been observing the lack of Franco-Indiennes returning to their motherland. More and more family homes are empty of life. Those who do live in Pondicherry aren't originally from here. 'Every two persons is from outside' and Sri Aurobindo Ashram is 'a city within a city', further segregating the tiny community. Feeling left out, Rayapoullé is happiest in her work, corresponding with scholars around the world, code-switching between Tamil, French and English as easily as she locates a French book of seventeenth-century maps of Pondicherry for me. Recommending additional reference texts about Pondicherry's cartography, botany, ecology, and for memoirs written by former French Governors, she points to the other end of the beach, where the French Institute stands. The two scholarly libraries bookend the Promenade, each building in between a title in Pondicherry's self-made encyclopaedia.

The French Institute of Pondicherry, or 'Institute' is busier than L'EFEO, and the security guard makes a show of signing everyone in and out. Inside, several hallways and doors lead library-seekers deeper into the building, as if into a temple's inner sanctum. Bags have to be left with the eager security guard and phones must be silenced, so after the sliding door to the library has been pulled shut, the air-conditioned air and silence feel imbued with something divine and quenching. This library is an ideal escape from the city's heat, especially for me, since my appointments and interviews tend to materialize at the last minute. The librarians request first-time browsers to fill out introductory forms and sign another log before helping them locate a book; once in the system, however, one is always welcome. The search engine technology looks less sophisticated than Samyuktha's acronym-filled university archives, but if a book is in the system, the moustachioed librarians will locate it.

167

Positioned at a table in the wake of both air conditioning and fan-fuelled breezes, I cool down enough to notice my seat mates: a man two generations older, steeped in a book about the history of Bharatanatyam; a petite Italian girl who has come to Pondicherry to study Sanskrit with a resident scholar. Conversation is discouraged, but the tables are small enough that everyone can see what everyone else is reading, or has left on the table to return to the next day. My pile includes *The Private Diary of Ananda Ranga Pillai*, whose detailed diaries of his time as dubash, or interpreter, for the French in the eighteenth century have since become a much needed Tamil perspective of colonial rule in Pondicherry; *Le Temps d'un Royaume,*

Rose Vincent's novel set in the same period, about the wife of Governor Dupleix; and François Martin's memoirs, which predate both Pillai and Madame Dupleix. Such book piles are scattered throughout the library, hinting at other projects being worked on.

The librarians keep busy, rotating periodicals, attending meetings on the second floor or taking tea breaks in the peaceful, lattice-sheltered courtyard out front. They are rigorous, as is evident in the questions they ask return visitors about their research interests— including those not noted in one's form, but discovered elsewhere. 'I found your website,' one librarian whispers to me conspiringly, and suggests more titles that might be relevant to me.

While the Institute's collections appear sparser than those at L'EFEO, the building hums with far more activity: active science experiments in the ecology labs on the ground floor; bilingual conferences taking place upstairs; students handling the Institute's treasured palm-leaf scrolls as they study the ancient messages etched onto them. Some of these are said to be Siddha Palm Leaf Manuscripts, and these young scholars are yet another echo to the era of siddhas and their unending pursuit of knowledge.

÷

Back at the Sri Aurobindo Ashram Archives, writings by and about Sri Aurobindo and the Mother dominate, but contributors end up writing about Pondicherry as well. I enjoy the travelogues written in the early twentieth century for the initial impressions that the colonial outpost have left on these Frenchmen. From naval officer Pierre Loti, in 1906, for example: 'In the center of Pondicherry there is a large, over-grown, and deserted square, ornamented in the middle by an elaborate fountain whose age does not, I think, exceed one hundred years, though the glare of the all-devouring sun has made it look much older. Somehow this open space conveys an impression of infinite sadness, though I am quite incapable of saying why.' And from writer and poet Maurice Magre, in 1936: 'The bazaar lies stretched out in the dust. At the doors of the shops, corpulent Mussalmans with thick lips offer their multi-coloured stuff. A canal divides the town in two, attesting by the filth which it drags with difficulty on its dead waters the eternal division of races. All along this canal, children play silently during the hours of day, and at night the phantom of cholera glides silently over the slime.'

The Ashram Library is managed by Shaupon Boshu, better known among the Ashram community as Shaupon da. Like L'EFEO and the Institute, this library also began in 1954. Although not located on the Promenade, it resides in an old French colonial building one block from the beach, and is tall enough to catch glimmers of blue sea from the first floor balcony. Walking in through the gates on Rue de St Martin, I am taken by the sight of gardens and a courtly, pillared portico. The Mother's vision that 'a library must be an intellectual sanctuary…[where] one should look for light and progress' has indeed been made manifest in this open-planned tree-lined structure. People are draped comfortably on staircases, at desks, in back hallways, and focused entirely on whatever they are doing. One visitor listens closely to a recording of classical music while another provides continuous commentary. A volunteer meticulously dusts and polishes one hard-bound book after another. Upstairs, opposite a long, open balcony, there is a central room full of busts and sculptures. Sri Aurobindo's bearded face greets the visitor first; behind him is a semi-circle of gods and goddesses in various poses, their tableau far more animated than the supramentalist's dreamy expression. A grandfather clock tick-tocks on a side wall, beyond which one spots the librarian at a table two rooms away.

170

He seems perfectly content to have his head buried in a book all day. But people are constantly approaching him for this or that, and Shaupon da engrosses each of them in conversation. It is near lunch time one afternoon but Shaupon da still shows me around the premises and asks, almost impatiently, as we're still settling into chairs at his corner table: 'Why are you here?' and 'What do you want from me?' The tone is immediately stark, honest, intimate—not surprising for a lifelong ashramite. Conversation weaves through Shakespeare, Melville, Faulkner, Sri Aurobindo's writings. Student volunteers start closing the doors to announce the afternoon lunch break, and as the rooms darken, goddess Parvati, standing in the gentle 'S' tribhanga position two rooms away, seems to be bent forward and listening to Shaupon da hold forth. For all the palm leaf study and research going on in the other libraries, it is on this conversation, I am thrilled, that a goddess has chosen to eavesdrop.

÷

Turning the corner from the Ashram Library, one ends up on Ranga Pillai Street, named after the indefatigable diarist. Starting closest to the beach and walking west, this street is, as the name suggests, full of books. First is the Romain Rolland Library, named after the French scholar who was a close friend of Gandhi's; its painted walls and shaded ledges make for pleasant outdoor seating when the library is closed for lunch. The library's AC Reading Room is the quickest to fill up: by 7 a.m. every day (except Monday, when the library is closed) the tube-lit room is full of white-shirt-and-lungi-wearing men combing through various newspapers in English and Tamil. Mobile phones do not ring; readers do not cough; there is only the occasional turning of a page. A side entrance to Romain Rolland leads to a Children's Library—an encouraging sign that such a small city stuffed with so many scholarly libraries still thinks about what books its children might enjoy reading.

Farther west from the library is the Pondicherry Museum, whose book collections are small but whose publications live in various other offices and libraries

171

in town. And farther still is the Ananda Ranga Pillai Museum, preserved in all its affluence since the house was first constructed in 1733, and today a three-dimensional representation of Pillai's extensive memoirs and memories.

Like its libraries, house-turned-museums are studded around Pondicherry's streets. Apart from Ananda Ranga Pillai's home, there is also the Subramania Bharati Museum. The archives are modest compared to the other libraries, but doctoral students studying Tamil literature, or Bharati's poetry and political writings travel here from all over the country. Prepared for long work days, they bring snacks which they keep carefully away from the reference texts they have spread around them on the floor. There are no chairs or desks in the museum; this is a house, after all.

÷

Turn left on Mission Street and the genre changes. The first Catholic press in South India is on this street, called Mission Press, and adjacent to the Immaculate Conception Cathedral. Built first in the mid-eighteenth century and again in the early nineteenth after the British had destroyed it, the press contains as much history and reverence as the church. While the printing press machinery is kept hidden away from the public eye in a large warehouse at the back, the front office is colourful with all sorts of Christian pamphlets.

Missionaries weren't Pondicherry's only eighteenth-century visitors. Susan S. Bean's *Yankee India: American Commercial and Cultural Encounters with India in the Age of Sail, 1784–1860* shares the rare story of the American ship *Empress of China* docking in Pondicherry in 1784—the very first contact the newly independent United States had made with this side of the world. Still close with their French allies, and with better timing than Le Gentil, they managed to reach India's southeastern coast when Pondicherry was very much a French territoire. Ship Surgeon Thomas Redman wrote in his journal:

> [We] passed close under the guns of the fort, with the 13 stripes flying which caused much speculation to the inhabitants what country our flag belonged to, as this was the first ship that ever hoisted the American colours on the coast of Coromandel... [The commandant, Marquis de Bussy] received us with the greatest demonstrations of pleasure and satisfaction and mentioned that every indulgence and privilege should be shewn our ship that a French ship was entitled to.

173

Like Maurice Magre, who arrived in Pondicherry over one hundred years later, Redman was simultaneously impressed with the town and aggrieved by its socio-economics:

> Pondicherry is one of the most healthy Settlements on this Coast, its situation is high and airy and

stands on a bank fronting on the sea... The town including the black one is near two mile[s] in length and about the same in depth, the white town is separated from the black by a canal... In the centre of the white town stands a most superb house, which is called the government house, where lives the commandant, it fronts an elegant parade which is planted all round with a double row of trees, forming delightful walks, and seats fixed at different parts of it, which [are] filled every evening with both sexes taking the air. The sun is so entirely hot during the day that you see no person in the street except those who are in their palanquins, which are carried by the black boys on their shoulders, which is the way you travel all through India. Here is the old observation made (if I mistake not) by Montesquieu that one half the world are born with saddles on their backs, and bridles in their mouths, for the other half to ride them to death.

For a more forgiving account of the ethnic French community in Pondicherry and how it endured the city's political and cultural changes, there is *A House in Pondicherry* by Lee Langley, who was born in Calcutta to Scottish parents, and now lives in London. The book had been out of print for over twenty years, so INTACH's Shubham Biswas tracked down the author, and then staged a 're-launch' of the book in Pondicherry in April 2018. The historical novel follows Oriane de l'Esprit from her precocious childhood to her wizened old age, all the while having lived at the same address on the fictional Rue Laval in the very real French Quarter. The only child of French parents, the protagonist spends her entire life in Pondicherry, accumulating Western viewpoints from her 'eastern horizon'. While Oriane rides in carriages and attends balls, she also suffers a near-lifelong heartbreak over a South Indian man.

Langley stages this simmering love story against a backdrop of several critical historical events in the town, from its colonial violence to the mysterious arrival of Aurobindo Ghose, from Indian Independence to the birth of Auroville ('Arcadia' in the novel). There is even a mention of Le Gentil. Langley depicts the city's growth in speedy paragraphs: 'What was once a village, a huddle of fishermen's huts on the Coromandel coast, had grown into a town regularly exchanged between warring nations, sometimes fought for, sometimes formally handed over...armies had arrived...the men nauseous or footsore, dreaming of France or England ...heavily-clad men with red, burnt faces.'

A little later, she summarizes Pondicherry's history with a condescending monologue delivered by a politician from Delhi:

> The Romans came to Arikamedu and they made some very nice pottery and after a while they went home. And the Mughals had a go at us

175

for a while but it didn't quite work, did it? And the Danes and the Portuguese and the Dutch and the British all moved in for the pickings. And of course you French. You were lucky, having your Revolution while you were here—our fellows felt very good about that: *liberté, egalité, fraternité*—even though your Capucins and Jesuits knocked down our temples and your judges didn't want our lawyers wearing shoes in court because it made them a bit too European for your liking... But even you people are only temporary residents, in due time we will ask you to leave.

Through the lenses of French and Tamil literature, and the arguments for and against French rule, Oriane develops thoughts and feelings in two languages, across two cultures, spanning the different quarters of Pondicherry. Having lived her whole life in the hotel her parents, and then she, ran, Oriane conceives of home as something that is both for insiders and outsiders; permanent and temporary; in demand and outdated. Through these clever contradictions, Langley narrates a colonial story and its aftermath while keeping l'histoire—which means both story and history in French—uniquely Pondicherrian.

÷

It is said that Sage Agastya was the original bibliographer in South India, and that when he settled in Vedapuri, sometime around 1000 BCE, he spread his ideas from student to student, each one retaining the chapters that most sparked their curiosities. The puri, or city, of Vedas was a 'center of Vedic learning', a dynamic marketplace trading in spiritual questions and answers about identity, existence, the divine. I am heartened to find that whether Agastya belongs to myth, history, or 'mythistory'—to borrow Peter Heehs' phrase—there exists and flourishes a culture of catalogues and collections in Pondicherry. Along with passionate, systematic curators who spend full days looking after them.

Perhaps, then, it is not the size of a city that should dictate how much literature and scholarship it encompasses. Rather, it is the city's allure for storytellers, its siddhic whispers, its polyglot curiosities, and its waves, which have been the conduit for 'voyageurs', fishermen's folk tales, marine messages and celestial signals. Which is why, millennia after Sage Agastya and his Vedic disciples were buried deep into the earth, Pondicherry still sings the siren song of rustling paper, cracking spines, scratching pens, and millions of narrators.

My Mother Tongues

In this book, I wanted to capture the essence of Pondicherry. I looked for words that would describe the city: Quaint. European. Holy. A pulsing heart. A union territory. A beach getaway. When those didn't suffice, I looked for metaphors. The visual ones were obvious: the city was a beach, forever revealing itself and covering up again. A graph paper of streets to study and socialize in, 'lane-wise'.

The aural ones were easy, too. Pondicherry was a language: a set of rules with exceptions to those rules, and pronunciation quirks to accommodate Latin and Dravidian sounds. A library spanning Vedic texts, a first-century Greek naval itinerary, as well as Tamil, French and English books.

Identity was another metaphorical drive. The city was an ashram with consciousness as its commerce, full of people wishing to find themselves—what Yuvaraj called 'thedal', the Tamil word for searching. More politically, Pondicherry was an 'option': an opportunity—or an accident—of nationality. A chance to start afresh or to stay put, to plant family trees oceans away, or remain rooted to the same earth.

But the Promenade wasn't my only vantage point from which to study my subject. Nor was I just its flâneuse. Turning off the beach onto Perumal Kovil Street, I became a granddaughter in search of her grandparents' first home in Pondicherry, curious about the house my father and his siblings grew up in. Located in the Tamil Quarter, the street is lined with thinnais, or front porches, beyond which are front doors leading inside homes. My grandparents had lived at Number 52, but given that the numbering scheme had changed at least once, I was doubtful of identifying the house correctly. It was the peak of summer and the sun was at its zenith. I marvelled at an old woman sitting on a plastic chair in front of her house, indifferent to the heat, resplendent in a purple sari and orange blouse, her wavy grey hair loose around her shoulders. On a whim, I approached her. I was looking for old Number 52; did she happen to know which one that was?

She looked westwards down the street. 'It's that way,' she said in Tamil. 'Go past the hotel, and go four, five houses down.'

I thanked her. And flush with something I can't explain—maybe the heat, maybe my family's stories—I added that my grandparents had once lived here, some fifty years earlier. 'My grandfather worked at the UCO Bank near Bharati Park.'

She nodded as if she had been expecting to hear

this. 'I remember him,' she continued. 'And his wife. Mathuram.'

She went on, as eloquent as someone who had been given a script; as nonchalant as someone who was asked about former neighbours on a daily basis. 'It was a rented place. They had five daughters. And one son, maybe two. He was good-looking. So was she. Only, she went grey at a young age. Maybe from having so many children. She sang well.' A pause. 'Yes, that's right; Mathuram.'

Hearing my late grandmother's name out of a stranger's mouth on a quiet street in a city I was just beginning to understand, I didn't know how to react. In that moment my father's childhood—until now the stuff of folklore and dreams—became three-dimensional.

I could picture my father and his brothers playing on that street. I could hear my aunts taking singing lessons nearby. I could keep pace with my father reciting French verb conjugations in front of his stern, suspicious teacher, whose memory still makes my father chuckle. I could smell the freshly baked bread that my grandfather brought home from the Ashram bakery; I could follow him on his bicycle to the lumberyard to pick out wood for the house he had built in Ilango Nagar, which is still standing today. I could feel the rush of wind as he sprinted to the train station and requested that the train departing to Villipuram wait a few more minutes for his relatives, who were running late. (It did.) I could map out my great-aunt's walk from the house to the beach, which she did every morning for months while mourning the death of a loved one. I could order Italian food at the rooftop restaurant where my uncle took his then-fiancée on their first date. I could hold my breath as my father and his friends dared each other to jump into the sea after school, even when none of them could swim properly. I could watch my aunts and uncles studying for the JIPMER entrance exams—three of them went on to become doctors. Pondicherry wasn't just a metaphor any longer. It was an heirloom. My great-grandfather had run the UCO Bank branch; my grandfather had worked there; my grandmother had raised eight children, and made enough of a racket that grey-haired Vatsala down the street still remembered them all.

I thanked her profusely and went on my way. Somewhere further down Perumal Kovil Street, it struck me that Pondicherry is the only city where my faux multilingualism makes sense. I understand and speak some Tamil because my parents are Tamil; I speak fluent English because I lived abroad; and I can get by in French because I studied it as a second language in school—and that too because my father had studied it, because he had grown up in what was then still a French colony in India. Which means that, more than New York City, my home for thirteen years, and more than Delhi, where I am now raising my daughter (and taking Hindi lessons), my desire and my ability to be most articulate is here, in Pondicherry.

Not just my family heirloom then, this city. Also my mother tongues.

Back on the Promenade, the sun is beginning to set, its rays slanted over the array of buildings we met in previous pages. The old distillery at the northern end of the beachfront, shut down twenty years ago, is quiet and deserted. The French consulate's rooftop, all gleaming solar panels, soak up the dwindling light. The white boxes painted on the road in front of the Ashram guest houses 'Sea Side' and 'Retreat' are empty; they will erupt with colour on Pongal, when women are invited to draw kolam designs in them, a colourfully competitive, light-hearted way to celebrate the spring harvest. I carry on until I reach Governor Dupleix, whose statue has been transported from the middle of the Promenade to a Children's Park at the southern end of the beach. This grassy trapezoid contains a maze of pathways populated with small stone statues of elephants and turtles. In the centre, Pondicherry's fifth Governor General keeps watch. His left index finger points downward, as if telling passers-by to stop and listen to his memoirs—and once they have, to follow his gaze, which is fixed upon the Promenade. Head north, it signals to me.

So I turn around for another lap. Now the buildings are on my left and the sea on my right. The beach, which has been visibly decreasing year by year, disappears behind a wall of stone tetrapods. They stand at attention, these concrete soldiers, on constant watch

182

against the next cyclone or tsunami. As formidable as they look, I imagine instead a sandy beach of the future, to be reconstructed by Sunaina Mandeen and her team. It seems appropriate to expect that this army of rock will someday be banished, like so many others who have washed up on the city's shores, spent some time, and then been cast back into ocean tides and trade winds.

As the tide comes in that evening, so do waves of walkers, creating a barricade between their town and the ocean. If Fort Louis once controlled both the sea and the hinterland, these evening walkers are equally vigilant, loyal, focused. This time on the beach rejuvenates some and calms others. Each group is different from the next: a line of young men stretched across the width of the road, scouting the crowd for attractive faces. A cluster of burkha- and niqab-clad women whisper past, their children jingling around them, anklets flashing in the evening sun. A man in a lungi walks erect, hands behind his back, a Walkman in his shirt pocket piping out Tamil film songs. Scuba divers, bodies toned from daily outings, point out various Pondicherry sights to the clients they are bringing back from a dive. Newlyweds hold hands, as much out of affection as for protection against being separated. Foreign accents and languages form a crepuscular layer of atmosphere: Tamil, English, Bengali, French, Italian, Odiya, Hindi, and their creole combinations bounce off the building facades and are swallowed up by the sea. Each is an account of Pondicherry's story, yes, but also a reminder that these variegated stories share this particular strip of land. And even if other cities have beachfronts, and even if other cities contain a diversity of people and cultures, Pondicherry is both old enough to contain multitudes *and* small enough to fit them on its beach.

And, now, although the sun has set, and the waves are heeding their lunar shepherd, the boules are still on the move. The game of Pondicherry is still in play.

Acknowledgements

My father's parents, for building a home and a life in Pondicherry. My mother's parents, for doing so in Chennai. Travelling from one to the other, on my many research trips for this book, I forged deeper connections with each one of them.

My husband, whose red pen saved my best ideas and sentences and spared you the rest, and who promised that my 'Alice in Wonderland' approach to the book would work. My daughter, who ensured she was born only after I had submitted my manuscript. My father, for all his stories about Pondicherry, and the love and verve with which he shared them; without him, there would be no book. My mother, for knowing when to ask about my progress, and when not to. My sister, for her unflagging excitement from beginning to end, and help with the final touches. My brother, for his playlists and his conversation, which made the writing process much more hypnotic. My uncles and aunts, who shared their memories of Pondy as well as their friends, many of whom (fed and) helped me in the city. My great-aunt, who politely and firmly insisted that we be allowed into the private chambers of the UCO Bank building; by the time we left, we were great friends of the AGM. My mother-in-law, who listened patiently when I called her after long days in the field, and knew exactly what to say. My father-in-law, for recommending

I read Ananda Ranga Pillai's diaries long before I knew who he was. My brother-in-law, for title suggestions. My sister-in-law, for her quiet support.

Shiv Subramaniam read my original proposal before I submitted it at 4 a.m., accompanied me to Pondicherry twice, and clarified my doubts about Sri Aurobindo. Pratap Bhanu Mehta suggested 'an opening which you can return to in the end as well', and naturally, he was right. Naresh Fernandes brainstormed with me at the beginning, and boosted my energy at the very end. Srinath Raghavan scanned pages out of his private archives for me to use. Priya Ramesh corrected my Tamil and improved chapter endings. Kamini Dandapani was cheerleader, editor, and colleague—all in one smiling personality. Parul Bhandari used her academic clout to find me reference books in Delhi. Anuja Kelkar helped translate all kinds of French: garbled iPhone recordings; archaic texts; and legalese. Janice Pariat wrote alongside me in apartments and cafés. Angela Lang reached Pondicherry shortly before I did, and her few-day-old friends there inaugurated my two-year-long interview journey. She, Jack Ryan and Aditya Iyer read drafts without complaining.

In Pondicherry, a whole ecosystem sprung into action without me realizing it, both within and beyond the boulevards. Yuvaraj Mani in the Tourism Office became my personal tour guide; half the interviews in this book are thanks to him. Debo Sahoo introduced me to Ashram personalities and took me to people's homes as his guest. Siva Mathiyazhagan's selfless work for youth in Pondicherry gave me access to the city's bravest, and humblest, advocates. Thribhuvan Manoharan gave me the thrill of watching a film from the projector room, and taught me how to understand a city through its movie halls. Akash Kapur took me to lunch and neither laughed at my narrative theories nor hesitated to share his contact list. Peter Heehs let me intrude on his sacred morning walks on the Promenade. P. Raja proofread my manuscript and knew the name of the woman selling coconuts on a quiet corner in Pondicherry; he is a true local. Indrani Cassime, by way of Shruti Narayan, opened up a whole Pondy quarter for me. Curtis John Degler hosted me in Mamallapuram and organized a snake-catching tour; something to cross off the bucket list. Dr Srinivasan walked me around JIPMER's campus for an entire afternoon; we met people who had known my family decades earlier. Prakash Nanwani was never fazed when I snuck into his shop on Nehru Street for air-conditioning, shade, and a cup of tea. Aneesh Raghavan was a friend and chauffeur, not to mention scholar, dancer, poet and singer; there was always room for me on the back of his bike. Shubham Biswas taught me about cultural heritage before going off to get a master's in it; I am grateful for all the books and notes he compiled for me. Lata Jauhar was my trilingual octogenarian encyclopaedia; she recognized people on every street, and gave me access to some of the city's oldest memories. Janakiraman Kothandapani infused the spirit of the city into his cover design.

Simar Puneet sparked the beginnings of this book. Pujitha Krishnan delivered the final result.

Notes

Prologue: A Game of Pétanque

xi   **The union territory pays tender homage:** M. Dinesh Varma and Annie Philip, 'Puducherry bursts into fireworks on Bastille Day', *The Hindu*, 15 July 2014.

xii   **'In protest, almost all the local population':** Diane E. Davis and Nora Libertun de Duren (eds.), *Cities and Sovereignty: Identity Politics in Urban Spaces*, Bloomington: Indiana University Press, 2011, pp. 47–48.

xii   **When he died in 1950, about 60,000 people:** 'Epilogue', Peter Heehs, *The Lives of Sri Aurobindo*, <https://www.aurobindo.ru/workings/other/peter_heehs-the_lives_of_sri_aurobindo_e.htm> [accessed: 17 December 2018].

xiii   **Pondicherry has one of the highest suicide rates in the country:** Annie Philip, 'Suicides refuse to go south', *The Hindu*, 29 July 2015.

xiii   **Even faraway *New York Times* has discussed:** Akash Kapur, 'Drowning in a sea of garbage', 22 April 2010.

xiii   **Pondicherry University students went on strike in 2015:** Sruthin Lal, 'Pondicherry University students intensify week-long strike', *Hindustan Times*, 3 August 2015.

xiii   **Sri Aurobindo Ashram was under investigation for harassment:** Harish V. Nair, 'Reports of women and children harassment put Aurobindo Ashram under SC scanner', *India Today*, 18 January 2015.

ONE: Maps and Metaphors

1   **two thousand years ago it was Poduke:** Raoul McLaughlin, *The Roman Empire and the Indian Ocean: The Ancient World Economy and the Kingdoms of Africa, Arabia and India*, Barnsley: Pen and Sword Military, 2014. Another book that mentions Poduke is William H. Schoff (trans.), *The Periplus of*

the Erythraean Sea: Travel and Trade in the Indian Ocean by a Merchant of the First Century, New York, London, Bombay and Calcutta: Longman, Green and Co., 1912.

1   **a dozen years ago it reincarnated into Puducherry:** 'Bill to rename Pondicherry as Puducherry passed', *The Hindu*, 22 August 2006.

2   **some scholars referred to it as Vedapuri:** 'History Of Puducherry', *Puducherry Smart City Development Limited* <https://pondicherrysmartcity.in/history-pondicherry.php> [accessed: 17 December 2018]. This is, however, not a unanimous opinion. Dr Jean Delcohe, a historian on Pondicherry, argues that Pondicherry was never known as Vedapuri. See Deepa H. Ramakrishnan, 'History in a new light', *The Hindu*, 15 April 2006.

2   **in their records they called it Puducheira:** 'Pondicherry from the origins to 1824', *Pondicherry Past and Present*, <http://www.ifpindia.org/digitaldb/site/pondicherry/data/part_1_introduction.html> [accessed: 17 December 2018].

2   **The Danes arrived twenty years later, in the 1630s:** Ibid.

2   **A Dutch map produced in 1690 announced their territory as Podechery:** Jean Deloche, *Origins of the Urban Development of Pondicherry According to Seventeenth-Century Dutch Plans*, Pondicherry: Institut Francais de Pondichery, 2004.

2   **Aurangzeb was about thirteen years into his political campaigns in the south:** Taymiya R. Zaman, 'A Hindu soldier's Aurangzeb', *The Wire*, 15 January 2016.

3   **when the territory was 'finally and definitively restored to France':** William F. S. Miles, 'Defective decolonization: the Pondichéry legacy', *Proceedings of the Meeting of the French Colonial Historical Society*, Vol. 16, 1992, pp. 142–53. JSTOR <www.jstor.org/stable/42952244> [accessed: 17 December 2018].

4   **with government descriptors like 'metropolitan region' and 'urban agglomeration':** 'Puducherry city census 2011 data' <http://www.census2011.co.in/census/city/495-puducherry.html> [accessed: 17 December 2018].

5   **These enclaves were jointly administered by the French as comptoirs:** Akhila Yechury, 'Imagining India, Decolonigizing L'Inde Francasie c. 1947-1954', *The Historical Journal*, Vol. 58, No. 4, Cambridge: Cambridge University Press, 2015, pp.1141–65.

5   **it quit the French dominion in 1949:** Miles, 'Defective decolonization'.

5   **Correspondingly, it carries a fainter presence of its colonial power:** Nirupama Subramanian, 'The forgotten French colony

of Chandernagore, an hour from Kolkata', *National Geographic Traveller India*, 3 May 2017 <http://www.natgeotraveller.in/the-forgotten-french-colony-of-chandernagore-an-hour-from-kolkata/> [accessed: 17 December 2018].

5   **Unlike the British departure from India:** Miles, 'Defective decolonization'.

5   **1962 as the year the year the Constitution was extended to Pondicherry:** 'De jure transfer day celebrated', *The Hindu*, 17 August 2013.

6   **The capital of the UT is the largest enclave:** 'Districts of Puducherry' <http://www.census2011.co.in/census/state/districtlist/puducherry.html> [accessed: 18 December 2018].

7   **the city has the oldest lycée, or French high school, outside of France:** 'Lycee Francais', *Pondy Tourism* <http://www.pondytourism.in/iconics-innerpage.php?id=40&district=Puducherry&category=195> [accessed: 18 December 2018].

TWO: A Landscape of Portraits

11   **'Transit of Venus', a rare sighting of the planet's orbit:** Shweta Krishnan, 'Missed tryst with transiting Venus', *The Hindu*, 5 June 2012.

11   **'geography owes its actual perfection...regarded as the true geographers':** Helen Sawyer Hogg, 'Out of old books (Le Gentil and the Transits of Venus, 1761 and 1769)', *Journal of the Royal Astronomical Society of Canada*, Vol. 45, p. 41, <http://adsbit.harvard.edu/cgi-bin/nph-iarticle_query?bibcode=1951JRASC..45...37S&db_key=AST&page_ind=4&plate_select=NO&data_type=GIF&type=SCREEN_GIF&classic=YES.> [accessed: 18 December 2018].

12   **'learned from the ships of this country':** Ibid.

12   **'to make all the observations that I could on geography':** Ibid., p. 42

12   **'compensated me to some extent':** Ibid.

12   **he reached Manila and was told that he could not stay:** Michael Wright, 'The ordeal of Guillaume Le Gentil', *Surreal Times*, 6 February 2012 <https://princetonastronomy.wordpress.com/2012/02/06/the-ordeal-of-guillaume-le-gentil/> [accessed: 18 December 2018].

13   **'All this excellent masonry of brick':** Hogg, 'Out of old books', p. 128.

13   **'I enjoyed at Pondicherry':** Ibid., p. 127.

13   'I had gone more than ten thousand leagues': Ibid., p. 132.

14   Built in 1836, the lighthouse: Ibid.

15   'The crowd is his element': Charles Baudelaire, 'The painter of modern life', Jonathan Mayne (ed. and trans.), *The Painter of Modern Life and Other Essays*, London: Phaidon Press, 1964, p. 9.

15   'opens his eyes to see': Ibid., pp. 10–11.

16   a lighthouse that has been dark for over forty years: 'Old light house', *Pondy Tourism* <http://www.pondytourism.in/iconics-innerpage.php?id=55&district=Puducherry&category=196> [accessed: 18 December 2018].

21   Before these streets were thoroughfares: 'Pondicherry from 1700-1761: urban expansion and defensive works', *Pondicherry Past and Present* <http://www.ifpindia.org/digitaldb/site/pondicherry/data/part_1_2.html> [accessed: 18 December 2018].

23   it was the Dutch who first imposed straight lines: Jean Deloche, *Origins of the Urban Development of Pondicherry According to Seventeenth Century Dutch Plans,* Pondicherry: Institut Francais De Pondichery, 2004.

24   Martin began constructing a high-walled 'fort': 'Du fort de Pondichery et des autres moyens de defense de la place', Francois Martin, Memoirs, Volume III.

24   In 1761, the English razed the French fort and churches: 'Pondicherry (1761-1778): reconstruction of the town, public buildings', *Pondicherry Past and Present* <http://www.ifpindia.org/digitaldb/site/pondicherry/data/part_1_4.html> [accessed: 18 December 2018].

25   a financial centre with a Dutch and then French coin mint: See 'Lot 277—Rare silver two royaliners coin of Pondicherry mint of India French', *Marudhar Arts*, https://www.marudhararts.com/printed-auction/auction-no-17/lot-no-277/coins-of-india/european-enclave/india-french/rare-silver-two-royaliners-coin-of-pondicherry-mint-of-india-french-.html; and 'The coin galleries: Dutch India', *Coin India*, <http://coinindia.com/galleries-dutch.html> [accessed: 18 December 2018]

25   Cercle de Pondicherry athletic club, franchises of which existed in Saigon and Hanoi: Pierre Brocheux and Daniel Hemery, *Indo China: An Ambiguous Colonization, 1858–1954*, Berkeley: University of California Press, 2011, p. 188.

26   'darting on to a sheet of paper': Baudelaire, 'The painter of modern life', pp. 11–12.

THREE: Water from a Whore

29   there is nothing besides a dry stone basin: From the key on p. 98 for the map of 'Pondicherry in 1891' in Raphaël Malangin, *Pondicherry that was Once French India*, New Delhi: Roli Books and INTACH, 2015.

30   'a physiological peculiarity—a thick growth of hair on his soles': P. Raja, *A Concise History of Pondicherry*, All India Books, 1987, p. 104.

30   'femme de joie': Ibid, p. 102.

31   The Siddha meditated awhile: P. Raja, *Water Please*, p. 40.

FOUR: Namma Bhaashai

48   the Cradle Baby Scheme launched by the Tamil Nadu government: 'How long will cradle baby scheme continue?', *The Hindu*, 30 November 2016.

51   'though these kids went as part of the Indian contingent': Olympia Shilpa Gerald, 'Lack of funds, facilities for APAC Special Olympics athletes', *The Hindu*, 15 November 2013.

51   Satya coughed up the Rs. 60,000 per athlete: 'Annual Report 2013/14', *Satya Special School* <http://satyaspecialschool.org/wp-content/uploads/2014/08/Annual-Report_2013-14.pdf> [accessed: 19 December 2018].

52   Vani, Dharun: Names changed.

57   Pondicherry in all its true sense: 'Welcome to Le Pondy', *Le Pondy Resort* <http://www.lepondy.com/> [accessed: 19 December 2018].

58   each boasts a neighbourhood 'poet and nationalist': S. Prasad, 'Bharati's home to be opened tomorrow', *The Hindu*, 4 February 2016.

59   'patriotic verses, poems on national integration and education': Indira Arjun Dev, Santo Datta and Arjun Dev (eds.), *Poems, Subramania Bharati: a Selection from Bharati's Poems in Tamil Original, Roman Transcription and English Translation*, New Delhi: National Council of Education and Training, 1982, p. v, <https://archive.org/stream/in.ernet.dli.2015.231768/2015.231768.Poems-Subramania_djvu.txt> [accessed: 19 December 2018].

59   'roam in the fields, absorbed in nature': Ibid., p. xi.

59   Bharati quit Chennai for Pondicherry: S. Vijaya Bharati, 'Annotated biography of C. Subramania Bharati', p. 8 <https://subramaniabharati.com/wp-content/uploads/2013/01/annotated-

biography1.pdf> [accessed: 19 December 2018].

59   **The vernacular magazine's motto was 'Liberty, Equality, Fraternity':** Indira Arjun Dev, Santo Datta and Arjun Dev (eds.), *Poems, Subramania Bharati*, p. xiii.

59   **Bharati had met fellow activists:** Ibid.

59–60   **The latter published Ghose just before he went into hiding in Bengal':** Bharati, 'Annotated biography of C. Subramania Bharati', p. 9.

60   **We shall swap the wheat:** Verses 6 and 7, 'Bharat Desh', Indira Arjun Dev, Santo Datta and Arjun Dev (eds.), *Poems, Subramania Bharati*.

61   **A 2009 edition of the poem:** Sri Aurobindo, *Savitri: A Legend and a Symbol*, New Delhi: Savitri Foundation, 2012.

61   **My countrymen!:** 'Allah' and 'Yesu Kiristu 'quoted in Indira Arjun Dev, Santo Datta and Arjun Dev (eds.), *Poems, Subramania Bharati*, p. 106 and 108.

62–63   **it is now a proud tribute to the house's Tamil and French architecture:** S. Prasad, 'Bharati's home to be opened tomorrow'.

FIVE: Called to Prayer

67   **It was most recently completed in 1791:** 'About the Cathedral', *Immaculate Conception Cathedral* <http://cathedralpondicherry.com/about-the-cathedral/> [accessed: 19 December 2018].

67   **The year 2017 marked the 325th anniversary:** Interview with Raj on 6 Jan 2017 and 'Immaculate Conception Cathedral', *Pondy Tourism* <http://www.pondytourism.in/iconics-innerpage.php?id=19&district=Puducherry&category=194>[accessed: 19 December 2018].

74   **a life-size replica of the Sanctuary of Our Lady of Lourdes:** *Lourdes Sanctuarie* <https://www.lourdes-france.org/en> [accessed: 19 December 2018].

75   **his grandfather H. M. Cassime was Mayor of Pondicherry:** 'H. M. Cassime', *Wikipedia* <https://en.wikipedia.org/wiki/H._M._Cassime> [accessed: 19 December 2018].

75   **C. M. Achraff...elected to the legislative assembly of Pondicherry in 1969:** 'Pondicherry 1969', *Latestly* <https://www.latestly.com/elections/assembly-elections/pondicherry/1969/bussy/> [accessed: 19 December 2018].

76   **'father was a Tamil-speaking, French-educated medical practitioner':** 'Introduction', Lourdes Tirouvanziam-Louis, *The Pondicherry Kitchen*, New Delhi: Westland Publishers, 2012.

77   'take up education in Pondicherry': http://www.clunyindia.org/
77   In 1987, he 'initiated'...the Inter-Religious Fraternal Community: Interview with Father A. S. Antonisamy on 11 January 2017.
78   today, is 87 per cent Hindu, and about 6 per cent Christian and 6 per cent Muslim: 'Puducherry population 2011', *Census 2011* <http://www.census2011.co.in/census/state/puducherry.html> [accessed: 19 December 2018].
78   He was so prolific in this new language: Patrizia Granziera, 'Christianity and Tamil culture: Father Joseph Beschi and the image of the Virgin Mary', *Toronto Journal of Theology*, Toronto: University of Toronto Press, Vol.27, No. 2, Fall 2011, pp. 249–66, accessed via *Project Muse* <https://muse.jhu.edu/article/449818/pdf> [accessed: 19 December 2018].
83   many from the Chola dynasty, over 600 years old: S. Senthalir, 'Chola site plays backdrop for Pondicherry Heritage Festival', *The Hindu*, 6 February 2017.
84   At various temples, he is shown seated: 'Horses of a little tradition', *Frontline*, 12 May 2017.
84   His shrines are also found in wilder settings: From the abstract of Eliza F. Kent, *Sacred Groves and Local Gods: Religion and Environmentalism in South India*, New York: Oxford University Press, 2013.

SIX: L'Option

87   '*The Hindu* wrote an article about him on 7 January 2016': Anne Philip, 'Lakshmi, the protagonist of French fiction'.
88   '[c]onsidered French whatever their religion or caste': Quote from p. 292 of Jaques Weber. 'Chanemougam, 'King of French India': Social and Political Foundations of an Absolute Power under the Third Republic', *Economic and Political Weekly*, Vol. 26, No. 6, 1991, pp. 291–302. *JSTOR*, <www.jstor.org/stable/4397309> [accessed: 20 December 2018].
89   'would end in reconstituting the Brahmanic social system': Ibid., p. 293.
89   'definitive and irrevocable for the renonçant himself': Ibid., p. 295.
90   '[o]ne of the most unfortunate decolonizing experiences': Miles, William F. S., 'Defective Decolonization: The Pondichéry Legacy', *Proceedings of the Meeting of the French Colonial Historical Society*, Vol. 16, 1992, p. 142, *JSTOR*, <www.jstor.org/stable/42952244> [accessed: 20 December 2018].

91   'le grand démantèlement': Ibid., p. 146.

91   The Treaty of Cession of the Territory of the Free City of Chandernagor: Ibid., p. 145.

91   Its autonomous status as a "Free City": Ibid., p. 146.

92   'would multiply and prosper as an alien community': Ibid., p. 148.

92   'loophole[s] haunting French consular officials in Pondicherry today': Miles cites this article from *Le Monde* to support his claim about loopholes in citizenship today. Jean de la Guerivière, 'Treize mille Indiens français victimes d'un accident de l'histoire', *Le Monde*, 10 January 1976.

92   He writes that it was prepared without 'l'attention necessaire': Quoted from Claude Arpi, *Il y a 50 ans...Pondichéry: L'intégration des Etablissements français en Inde; Perspectives historiques et culturelles*, Auroville: Auroville Press Publishers, 2004, Fourth edition: 2016, p. 69.

93   Instead, there was a notice posted in the consulate: Ibid.

94   They were aware of what to do, and by when; their rural and remote counterparts: Ibid.

96   'history and the contribution of these French trained doctors': V., Nallam, *History of Medicine in French India*, Pondicherry: Mission Press, 2014, pp. 14 and 17.

97   This led to a proliferation of le 'résidence fictive': Arpi, *Il y a 50 ans...Pondichéry*, p. 71.

98   'it is a symbol of many things': Jawaharlal Nehru, *Selected Works of Jawaharlal Nehru*, Second Series, Vol. 27, 1 October 1954–31 January 1955, accessed from AIR tapes, NMML.

98–99 'continue to be a seat in many ways of the French language': Nehru, *Selected Works of Jawaharlal Nehru*.

99   '[w]e have looked at the world through British spectacles...give us': Foreword by Jaques Weber in Ajit K. Neogy, *Decolonization of French India: Liberation Movement and Indo-French Relations, 1947-1954*, Pondicherry: Institut Français de Pondichéry, 1997.

102   Nehru had envisioned Pondicherry as a 'fenêtre ouverte sur la France': 'Amaigri, fatigué, j'arrive à Pondichéry, la française', *Le Monde*, 6 August 2009.

SEVEN: A Supramental Life

105   'some 4,600 pages of philosophy, commentary, translations': Peter Heehs, *The Lives of Sri Aurobindo*, Fn995, <https://www.aurobindo.ru/workings/other/peter_heehs-the_lives_of_sri_

aurobindo_e.htm#995_> [accessed: 20 December 2018] .

106 In 1922, a French woman named Blanche Rachel Mirra Alfassa: name from Bindu Mohanty's essay, in Akash Kapur, *Auroville: Dream and Reality: An Anthology*, Gurgaon: Penguin Books, 2018, p. 298.

106 'an oceanic flood of Light rushing down from above': Heehs, *The Lives of Sri Aurobindo*, Fn1057.

106 '"the Ananda" or plane of cosmic bliss had "descended in the physical"': Ibid.

106 By the end of 1926, Ghose had become Sri Aurobindo to his devotees: Ibid.

107 'Mirra is my Shakti': Sri Aurobindo, reported oral remarks according to notation of 27 November 1926, *Haradhan Bakshi Papers*, Notebook 3, 240, in SAAA.

108 What the supramental will do the mind cannot foresee or lay down: Sri Aurobindo, *Letters on Yoga*, Vol. 1, Part 1, <https://www.aurobindo.ru/workings/sa/22/0001_e.htm>; Sujata Nahar, Michel Danino, Shankar Bandopadhyay, eds., *Sri Aurobindo to Dilip*, 4 Volumes, First edition, Vol. 1, 1929 – 1933, Pune: Heri Krishna Mandir Trust; Mysore: Mira Aditi, 2003, p. 384.

109 'One has to pass beyond and supramentalise overmind': Sri Aurobindo, *Letters on Yoga*, p. 257 and 263.

109 Its "descent", that is, its manifestation in the physical world: Heehs, *The Lives of Sri Aurobindo*, Fn1057.

109 In the late 1940s, Sri Aurobindo's revised and collected chapters: Publisher's note in *The Life Divine*, Pondicherry: Sri Aurobindo Ashram Publication Department, 2005.

109 'aura of light around the body': Heehs, *The Lives of Sri Aurobindo*, Fn1057.

114 In *The Ideal of Human Unity*, which Sri Aurobindo first published: Quoted from the Publisher's Note in *The Ideal of Human Unity*, Lotus Press, July 2010.

114 '[h]istory teaches us nothing; it is a confused torrent of events and personalities: *Ideal of Human Unity*, p. 9.

116 'Ideas sometimes leap out as armed forces': Ibid., p. 127.

117 'sent shock waves throughout the community of thousands of devotees': Quoting the judgment 'Sri Aurobindo Ashram Trust and Ors Vs. R. Ramanathan and Ors', <http://courtverdict.com/supreme-court-of-india/sri-aurobindo-ashram-trust-and-ors-vs-r-ramanathan-and-ors> [accessed: 20 December 2018].

117 'to ensure that there should be no publication of the objectionable book': Ibid., No. 15.

117   'every copy of the objectionable book, its copies, reprints': Ibid., No. 16.

117   Russian-hosted website titled 'Site of Sri Aurobindo & The Mother': Heehs, *The Lives of Sri Aurobindo*.

118   'The Aurobindo that interests me is the one who turned': Peter Heehs, 'Getting beyond the Conventions of Biography—and Hagiography Too', *Columbia University press Blog*, 4 August 2008 <http://www.cupblog.org/?p=343> [accessed: 20 December 2018]

121   'clothes, toiletries and other necessary commodities': *Sri Aurobindo Ashram*: 'Organisation', *Sri Aurobindo Ashram* <https://www.sriaurobindoashram.org/ashram/organisation.php> [accessed: 21 December 2018].

121   'which include farms, gardens, healthcare, guesthouses': 'Departments', *Sri Aurobindo Ashram* <https://www.sriaurobindoashram.org/ashram/departments.php> [accessed: 21 December 2018].

121   But the ashram's revenue mostly comes from donations and the ashramites: Jayanti Parekh, 'The Sri Aurobindo Trust and its Administration', Well-wishers of Sri-Aurobindo Ashram, <https://wellwishersofsaa.wordpress.com/2015/03/14/thesri-aurobindo-ashram-and-its-administration-by-jayantilal-parekh/> [accessed: 21 December 2018].

123   'I don't know a town this size in India that is as cosmopolitan': Ibid.

EIGHT: Inheritance

126   Or perhaps because it has been written about by Indian, French and British archaeologists: 'Erythraean Sea Trade', <http://www.wou.edu/history/files/2015/08/Joshua-Hall-HST-499.pdf> [accessed: 21 December 2018].

127   Some of their findings have been installed at the Pondicherry Museum: A. Srivathsan, 'Setting the record straight on the Arikamedu finds', *The Hindu*, 1 July 2011.

128   Arikamedu and Nagapattinam are excavations and the remaining nine: 'List of Monuments and Sites: Puducherry Sub-circle', <http://asichennai.gov.in/downloads/puducherry-sub-circle-monuments-sites.pdf> [accessed: 21 December 2018].

130   'environmental awareness and civic consciousness': 'Seeds of Change', *PondyCan*, <http://pondycan.org/seeds-of-change/> [accessed: 21 December 2018].

133   'At least thirty metres of beach have been lost': Akash Kapur, 'Letter from Pondicherry, India', *Granta* <https://granta.com/letter-from-pondicherry/> [accessed: 21 December 2018].

133   The book came out in 2012 but his pictures feature a Pondicherry: Sebastian Cortés, *Pondicherry*, New Delhi: Roli Books, 2012, p. 23, 25, 28.

133   His shots show a much more spacious beach than today's version: Ibid., p. 111.

133   or room for crowds to gather and immerse idols during; Ibid., p. 137.

134   'this narrow strip of land has turned its back on the ocean': Pascal Bruckner, 'C'est un paradis exigeant', *Pondicherry*, p. 11.

135   After Pondicherry's government approved the building of a new port: Sumana Narayanan, 'Puducherry port in deep water', *Down to Earth*, 4 July 2015.

135   filed a case in the Madras High Court to reverse the decision: R. Sivaraman, 'Government wins port project case', *The Hindu*, 1 August 2016.

135   When the high court dismissed the group's request, Villianur Iyarkai Padukappu Maiyam: 'Civil Appeal No. 3572 of 2009', *India Environmental Portal*, <http://www.indiaenvironmentportal.org.in/files/pondicherry.pdf> [accessed: 21 December 2018].

135   Undaunted, Pondicherry's environmentalists applied pressure: Sivaraman, 'Government wins port project case', *The Hindu*.

137   'history of the Pondicherry Port dates back to the tenth century A.D': 'Civil Appeal No. 3572 of 2009', p. 5.

138   During the 2018 festival, children were received in the French Consulate garden: S. Senthalir, 'Experiencing heritage through colouring', *The Hindu*, 15 February 2018.

138   Ashok Panda, Co-Convener of INTACH Pondicherry, and with the team: 'About us', *INTACH* [accessed: 21 December 2018].

140   In 2017, Pondicherry was selected by the central government: PTI, 'Puducherry included in Centre's smart city abhiyan', *Indian Express*, 23 June 2017.

140   as one of 100 cities to be developed into 'Smart Cities': 'Smart City Features', *Smart Cities Mission*, <http://smartcities.gov.in/content/innerpage/smart-city-features.php> [accessed: 21 December 2018].

141   'achieve urban economic and environmental goals': 'Meet on Asia Urbs in Pondy from today', *The Hindu*, 28 July 2004.

141   The Smart Cities Mission addresses three needs for any urban

space: 'Strategies', *Smart Cities Mission*, <http://smartcities.gov.in/content/innerpage/strategy.php> [accessed: 21 December 2018].

142 Mandeen recalls a festival event from a few years ago, organized by Justice Annoussamy: 'Retired Madras High Court judge Justice David Annoussamy will...Indian Pondicherry', *Times of India*, 5 August 2015.

NINE: Also Known As

146 'WiFi available BUT to initiate the concept': 'Café', *La Casita*, <http://lacasitaindia.com/travellers-cafe-pondicherry/> [accessed: 21 December 2018].

147 On 1 April 2016, 'International Rueda de Casino Flash Mob Day': S. Senthanil, 'Salsa surprise for visitors at the beach', *The Hindu*, 3 April 2016.

151 Akash Kapur, an Aurovilian since childhood and an internationally published author: Kapur, *Auroville: Dream & Reality*, Gurgaon: Penguin Books, 2018, p. xiii.

151 'representatives of 124 nations and 23 Indian states placed': Ibid., p. 297.

152 Over 2,500 people from about fifty countries: Ibid., p. xvi.

152 'Aren't we here to try and create a model society': Rishi Walker, 'Hasta La Victoria Siempre', *Auroville*, p. 188.

152 'We are here to grow in consciousness, not build a city.': Anu Majumdar, 'An Eco Village?', *Auroville*.

152 'elusive, elliptical, tenaciously inconsistent': Ibid., p. xxii.

152 'vastly complex process in which diverse individuals': Alan Herbert, 'Something to Celebrate', *Auroville*, p. 135.

153 Call it a 'City of the Future': David Wickenden, 'The Living Laboratory', *Auroville*, p. 20.

153 'a medium of exchange only with the outside world': Bindu Mohanty, 'Background and Context on Auroville', *Auroville*, p. 301.

153 'A City of Yoga': Rud Lohman, 'A City With A Soul', *Auroville*, p. 89.

153 'work five hours daily for the common good': Bindu Mohanty, 'Background and Context on Auroville', *Auroville*, p. 301.

153 'City of Immortality': Vijay (Vittorio Gresele), 'The City and the Oasys', *Auroville*, p. 300.

153 'belongs to humanity as a whole': 'In the Words of the Mother the Auroville Charter', *Auroville*.

153   'personal resources, donations and grants': Bindu Mohanty, 'Background and Context on Auroville', *Auroville*, p. 298.

153   'it is easy to decry the threads rising': Raymond Thépot, 'Paradox-Town', *Auroville*, p. 98.

153   'I always had a sense of being surrounded by natural poets': Kapur, 'Introduction', *Auroville*, p. xix.

154   'collaboration and real brotherhood': Ibid., p. xxiv.

154   'bring about developments that are not always in keeping with the community's ideals': Ibid., p. 302.

154   One of the essay titles sums it up best: a 'Paradox Town': Ibid., p. 97.

160   Librarie Kailash (librarie in French means bookshop, not library) stocks books: French quotes taken from 'La maison d'édition', *Editions   Kailash*,   <http://www.editionskailash.com/Default. aspx> [accessed: 21 December 2018].

162   in a photobook of Pondicherry heritage homes: Gabriel Duval and and Jean-Claude Cuinat-Guerraz, *Pondichéry: Histoire d'un Comptoir,* Pondicherry: Le Lycée français of Pondicherry, 1996.

162   'bohemian-chic, New Age-meets-Old World hang-out': 'Welcome to Puducherry (Pondicherry)', *Lonely Planet,*<https://www. lonelyplanet.com/india/tamil-nadu/puducherry-pondicherry/ introduction> [accessed: 21 December 2018].

169   From naval officer: Chitleen K Sethi, 'Personalised travelogue', *The Tribune*, 15 September 2002.

169   'In the center of Pondicherry there is a large, over-grown': Pierre Loti, *India*, translated by George A. F. Inman, Chapter 4, Section 11, 'At Pondicherry', London: T. Werner Laurie Ltd, 1928, p. 133. (courtesy Ashram Archives)

169   'The bazaar lies stretched out in the dust.': Maurice Magre, 'L'Ashram de Pondicherry', *A La Poursuite de la Sagesse*, Paris: Fasquelle Editeurs, 1936. (courtesy Ashram Archives)

169–70 'a library must be an intellectual sanctuary: 'Departments', *Sri Aurobindo Ashram* <https://www.sriaurobindoashram.org/ ashram/departments.php> [accessed: 21 December 2018].

172   The first Catholic press in South India is on this street, called Mission Press: 'Streetscapes and Architectural Land marks', *Pondicherry   Past   and   Present*,   <http://www.ifpindia.org/ digitaldb/site/pondicherry/data/part_2_1_2_missionpress.html> [accessed: 21 December 2018].

173   Pondicherry is one of the most healthy Settlements: Bean, pp. 33-34.

175   'What was once a village, a huddle of fishermen's huts': Lee